Cover design by Scott Pryor, son of the author.
His email is scottwpryor@gmail.com

Little Known Tales In Sacramento History

Alton Pryor

Stagecoach Publishing
5360 Campcreek Loop
Roseville, CA. 95747
(916) 771-8166
www.stagecoachpublishing.com
stagecoach@surewest.net

Little Known Tales

In

Sacramento

History

ISBN: 978-0-692-26704-2

Library of Congress Control 2014947415

Alton Pryor

Men are afraid to rock the boat in which they hope to drift safely through life's currents, when actually, the boat is stuck on a sandbar. They would be better off to rock the boat and try to shake it loose.

Thomas Szasz

Table of Contents

Chapter 1

Sutterville

Sutter's fort at the junction of Sacramento and American rivers.

John Sutter built a wharf—the Embarcadero—on the Sacramento River, just south of its junction with the American River in 1839.

It was here, where Front and I streets intersect today, that he received supplies to restock Sutter's fort, located two and one-half miles away.

A sandbar sat in the way of navigation at the point where the I Street Bridge is located today. The sandbar hampered navigation except during periods of high water.

Sutterville was laid out by Lansford Hastings and John Bidwell. The town was first called Suttersville and changed to Sutterville in 1844. In exchange for laying out the town, Hastings and Bidwell each received a share of the lots that were to be sold.

John Sutter, Sr.

Sutter chose the site because it was on higher ground than the embarcadero and safer from the annual flooding of the Sacramento River.

Sacramento's history really began in 1839 when Mexican Governor Juan Alvarado gave John Sutter a 48,000 acre land grant. Sutter hoped to create a haven for European Swiss immigrants.

12

Sutter's fort was the first non-Native American community in the California Central Valley. Sutter built it as an agricultural and trading colony in *Mexican Alta California.*

Sutter's fort became most famous for its rescue efforts of the Donner Party which was stranded at the top of the Sierra Nevada mountain range.

Sutterville was popular as a trading depot. It contained one of the first brick buildings in California. This was a hotel built by George Zins in 1847.

The Sutterville post office operated from 1855 to 1860.

After the discovery of gold in 1848, the Embarcadero became a more desirable location for a commercial center because of its proximity to Sutter's fort and the roads to the mines.

Sutter's son, John Sutter, Jr., who came to California to help his father get out of debt, contracted with Captain William A. Warner and Lieutenant William Tecumseh Sherman to survey a new City of Sacramento.

He also contracted with Samuel Brannan, who owned a store at Sutter's fort, and with Peter H. Burnett to sell lots in the new city for $500 each to pay off his father's debt. Some of the lots that were further removed from the city's center were sold for $250 each.

Sutterville continued as a significant settlement. It was incorporated into the city of Sacramento in 1950. Today, it is preserved as a historical monument at the Sutterville Bend in the Sacramento River and Sutterville Road.

Chapter 2

Founding Sacramento

Sacramento City in 1850.

J ohn Augustus Sutter, Sr., abandoned his family in Switzerland to avoid debtor's prison. Sutter arrived in *Alta California* in grand style.

While transitioning between St. Louis and Santa Fe, Sutter lived in Westport (now Kansas City) where he learned of bucolic Mexican-owned California. The rumored opportunities for settlers were boundless.

It took many months before Sutter arrived in California. He first took an overland journey to Fort

Vancouver on the Columbia River. He then boarded a trading vessel to the Sandwich Islands (Hawaii) in hopes of connecting with a California-bound ship.

He was stranded in Honolulu for five months. He arranged to deliver cargo to San Francisco Bay on the ship *Clementine* on the condition that he could first make a delivery to the Russian outpost at Sitka, Alaska.

J Street in Old Sacramento.

Sutter arrived in Yerba Buena (now San Francisco) in July 1839. He was refused permanent admission to the harbor and told to sail to the official port of entry at Monterey.

Sutter arrived at Monterey, the colonial capital of California, near penniless. He disembarked with trunks of books and clothing, along with a big load of dreams.

He met with Alta California's Mexican governor, Juan Bautista Alvarado and convinced him of his grandiose plans for a settlement in California's interior. By marrying a Mexican woman, he was able to secure a 48,000 acre Mexican land grant.

By granting Sutter the land, it allowed Alvarado to secure the region without committing extra troops.

Sutter sailed up the Sacramento River with his little crew in two small sailing vessels and a pinnace (a light boat carried aboard trading vessels). He wanted to go far enough inland to avoid official surveillance and interference.

He found a spot of land on a rise near the confluence of the Sacramento and American Rivers.

It was there, a year after arriving, that he built Sutter's Fort, with its 18-foot tall adobe walls. He called the community New Helvetia. Translated, New Helvetia means "New Switzerland".

John Sutter, Sr.

Before the arrival of the Europeans, the Nisenan branch of the Native American Maidu Indians inhabited the area.

The Spanish were the first Europeans to explore the area. The area that is now Sacramento was deemed unfit for colonization by a number of explorers. As a result, the area remained untouched by the Europeans.

The first European in what is now California was conquistador Juan Rodriguez Cabrillo, a Portuguese explorer sponsored by the Spanish empire.

It was Gabriel Moraga, the first European to enter the Sierra who named the Sacramento River, although he incorrectly placed the rivers in the region.

Sutter controlled the area of his large land grant with a private army and with relative autonomy from the new and independent Mexican government.

Sutter was a grand success. He owned a ten-acre orchard and a herd of thirteen thousand cattle. Fort Sutter was a regular stop for the increasing number of immigrants arriving in California.

Sam Brannan rushed to open a store on the Sacramento River waterfront. It was then called Sutter's Embarcadero. The area was prone to flooding. It was victim to repeated fires consuming the hastily-built buildings that were constructed of wood and canvas.

Unlike other settlements, Sacramento City did not have gambling houses and saloons until the summer of 1849. The city was free of those types of businesses for the first few months of its existence.

Churches began to appear when pastor W. Grove Deal held services in the Methodist Episcopalian church in 1849. Catholic Reverend Augustine Anderson arrived in 1850 and built a church in 1854.

Edward C. Kemble, of San Francisco, moved north and established Sacramento's first newspaper, *The Placer Times.* Kemble was stricken with sickness three months later and the newspaper disbanded.

In 1847, Sutter hired James Marshall to build a saw mill which would allow him to expand his already-growing empire. Marshall selected a site for the mill at Coloma, which was situated on the American River.

While checking the tail race at the saw mill that was still under construction, Marshall spotted flakes of gold in the sandy gravel. He informed Sutter, who urged him and his other saw mill employees to keep the knowledge quiet until the saw mill was completed.

Sutter's colony grew as more and more pioneers came west. It was these same pioneers, most of whom were trappers, traders and gold rush miners, who spelled the biggest problem for Sutter.

Sutter's management skills had not improved with his arrival in America. He came to California, only to get himself into great debt again.

The new pioneers squatted on his property and his efforts to dislodge them seemed futile.

Sutter transferred some of his land holdings to his son, John Sutter, Jr., even though his son, who was still in Switzerland, was an underage minor, and not eligible to receive such holdings.

When John Sutter Jr. arrived in California, he found his father's business was disorganized and he was heavily in debt.

Sutter, Jr. was raised by his mother, Anna. He was put through "counting school" before he joined his father in California.

When young Sutter arrived, he found his father's business disorganized and in need of strong management. Soon after Sutter, Jr. arrived, his father left for Coloma where he hoped to sell mining supplies to the hundreds of gold prospectors flooding the area.

Even though the senior Sutter had plans for a town he would call Sutterville, his son had a different view. He would build a town at the fork of the American and Sacramento Rivers, which at the time was called Sacramento City.

In January 1850, a major flood ravaged the ground on which the city of Sacramento stood. The American and the Sacramento rivers crested simultaneously and the Embarcadero washed away in the flood.

Hardin Bigelow, the city's first elected mayor, advocated building the first levees and dams to guard Sacramento from future floods.

Bigelow remained in office for seven months before succumbing to cholera.

In 1853, a mammoth project was proposed to raise the new-born city above the flood level. This proposal wasn't fully accepted. It took another flood which devastated the area in 1862 to open the eyes of officials.

Within a few years, thousands of cubic yards of earth were brought in by wagons to raise the level of the streets. The original level can still be seen under the board walks in Old Sacramento.

The center of the commercial district of Sacramento City gradually moved eastward and the city on Sutter's Embarcadero became one of the worst skid row areas west of Chicago.

Reformers, ministers, politicians and others railed against the degraded community, but little was done to change the slum's basic condition.

A strain developed between John Sutter senior and junior. The son soon became ill and rarely left the family residence at "Hock Farm", located on the Feather River.

His illness continued and Sutter, Jr., became tired of his responsibilities. He wanted to sell his holdings, but figured they were too vast to sell. Some Sacramento businessmen, including the conniving Sam Brannan, heard about Sutter's, Jr.'s desire to sell.

The businessmen drew up a contract and urged young Sutter to sign and get out of California and go where the climate was more suitable to his condition.

Sutter, Jr., read the terms, and was not happy with them. Under pressure from Brannan and the other businessmen, he reluctantly signed the agreement.

Young Sutter moved to Acapulco, Mexico where he married Carmen Rivas. They had a son, John Sutter III. During this time, he was involved in court cases over the sale of his property to Brannan and the lack of payment for the property.

These court cases did not benefit Sutter, Jr., except to release him from the burden of caring for the estate.

In Acapulco, he worked in a small general store. When the principal owner died, Sutter took his share of the business. The business did so well that Sutter, Jr. was able to build a house near the ocean.

In 1865, he became the Vice-Commercial Agent for the Port of Acapulco. At the urging of friends, U.S. President Ulysses Grant named Sutter, Jr., U.S. consul in Acapulco.

Sutter, Jr. died in Acapulco, Mexico on September 21, 1897. He was originally interred in Acapulco, but was reinterred in the Sacramento Historic City Cemetery in Sacramento at the request of his daughter, Anna Sutter Young.

Chapter 3

The Sacramento River

The Sacramento River

The Sacramento River is the largest river in California and is situated almost entirely within California's boundaries. Its entire basin lies between the Sierra Nevada and the Cascade Range.

By discharge, the Sacramento River is the second-largest contiguous U.S. river draining into the Pacific. It is second to the Columbia River. The Pit River is the longest tributary of the Sacramento River.

Spanish sea captain Gabriel Moraga, 39-years-old, trekked up the big river on horseback. He was struck by the scene. Canopies of oaks and cottonwoods, festooned with grape vines, overhung both sides of the mighty stream.

Es Como el sagrado Sacrment!, Moraga exclaimed. (This is like the Holy Sacrament!) Thus the mighty Sacramento River got its name. Moraga followed the Sacramento north and camped on the banks of the Feather River.

The explorer mistakenly took the Feather River for the upper extension of the Sacramento. Causing his confusion was that at the junction of the Sacramento and Feather rivers, the wide Feather River aligns with the Sacramento below the junction. The narrower upper Sacramento angles in from the west at this point.

The main stem of the Pit River is 207 miles long and some water in the system flows 315 miles to the Sacramento River. Few rivers in the west have a more controversial name than the Pit River. There are some who say the stream is not entitled to a name at all as it is just an extension of the Sacramento River and should thus be called the "Upper Sacramento".

Another explorer, Captain Edward Belcher, of the British Navy, explored the Sacramento. He ordered his sailors to cut down several huge oak trees to measure them. One had a trunk 27 feet across.

The Pit River got its name from trappers of the Hudson Bay Company, who wandered around the area in search of good pelts. The trappers were amazed by the many "blind" holes dug by local

23

Indians to catch wild animals. They understandably dubbed the river the "Pit River".

By geologic standards, the Sacramento River is considered a "young" river. The borders of its watershed began to form only a few million years ago as magma welling up below the Earth's crust pushed up the Pacific Plate. As the Pacific Plate collided with the North American Plate, it formed the Sierra Nevada.

It is believed that the Sacramento River once had its outlet in Monterey Bay. The Monterey Bay outlet and the Sacramento and San Joaquin rivers were blocked off about two million years ago.

The runoff from the Sierra began to transform the Central Valley into a gigantic lake. This lake was called Lake Clyde.

Lake Clyde stretched 500 miles north to south and was at least 1,000 feet deep. About 650,000 years ago, the lake overflowed, draining into San Francisco Bay and creating the Carquinez Strait.

The Carquinez Strait is the only break for hundreds of miles in the Coast Ranges. The narrow outlet trapped some of the sediments of the rivers in the Central Valley, forming the Sacramento-San Joaquin Delta.

The Sacramento River and the Sacramento Valley was the center for the American Indian populations of California. Most of the villages were small. The original natives lived more as bands, or family groups, rather than as tribes.

The Sacramento Valley was settled about 12,000 years ago, but permanent villages only date back about 8,000 years. Historians have organized the original native groups into several "tribes". These include Shasta, Modoc, and Achomawi/Pit River Tribes.

The city of Sacramento flourished as the center of an agricultural empire that fed the thousands of gold miners.

By the late 19th century, California experienced an economic boom that led to the rapid expansion of both agriculture and urban infrastructure. The Central Valley was heavily developed as a farming region.

The cities along the state's Pacific coast and the Sacramento and San Joaquin rivers grew rapidly. This meant the waters of the raging rivers must be managed to prevent flooding.

As early as 1870, the U.S. Army Corps of Engineers and the state of California had detailed the geography and water supplies of the Sacramento, Feather, Yuba and Bear rivers.

In 1873, Colonel B.S. Alexander, of the Army Corps of Engineers, wrote about taking water from the water-rich Sacramento River basin into drought-prone South and Central California.

The California State Water Project and the Central Valley Project emerged during the Great Depression years of the 1930s.

Both began as the brain child of the state government. Because of the lack of funds, construction work and costs were shifted to the federal U.S. Army Corps of Engineers.

Construction of Shasta Dam, the main dam on the Sacramento River, started in 1938 and was completed in 1945. This dam was capable of absorbing enormous flood flows and could store the water for use during prolonged drought periods.

"The future of California is joined at the hip with the Sacramento River." (University of California Geologist Jeff Mount)

A natural added benefit was the navigation and electricity it gave the inhabitants of the Sacramento Valley.

The success of the Shasta Dam led to more dams being built on Sacramento's main tributaries, the Pit, Feather and American rivers. Folsom Dam, Oroville Dam and New Bullards Bar Dam were built in the 1900's and 1960s.

This brought the Sacramento River's flows under control. After the river's flow was under control, two major canals serving the western side of the Sacramento Valley—the Tehama-Colusa and Corning Canals were built.

●The Sacramento River is the largest river and watershed system in California.

●The Sacramento River is the second largest U.S. river draining into the Pacific. The Columbia River is first.

26

●The Sacramento River carries thirty-one percent of the state's total surface water runoff. Its primary tributaries are the Pit, Feather and American rivers.

●The Sacramento River Basin provides drinking water for residents of northern and southern California, supplies farmers with water and is vital for sustaining California's wildlife system.

Chapter 4

The Great Flood of 1862

The great flood of 1862 devastated downtown Sacramento.
The above lithography is on K Street in Sacramento.

T he rain began on November 8, 1861 and for four weeks it didn't let up. It was the largest flood in the recorded history of Oregon, Nevada and California.

Throughout the affected area, all the streams and rivers rose to great heights, flooded the valleys and inundated or swept away towns, mills, dams, flumes, houses, fences and domestic animals. It ruined agricultural fields.

One-quarter of the taxable real estate in California was destroyed in the flood. Since it was dependent on property taxes, the State of California went bankrupt.

The governor, the state legislature and state employees were not paid for a year-and-a-half.

The year 1862 is used as the model year by flood planners to prepare against another such devastating event. The official name pinned on the event was "The Arkstorm", but unofficially, it is simply called, "The other big one!"

The entire Sacramento and San Joaquin valleys were inundated for 300 miles long and 20 miles wide. John Carr, of Weaverville, witnessed the sudden snow melt by the heavy rain which set off the flooding.

The winter of 1861 was a hard one. From November until the latter part of March there was a succession of storms and floods. I remember my being in Weaverville. It had been raining all the day previous.

We arrived at the ranch and I wanted to cross the bridge and stay at John Carter's that night, but Uncle Sturdivant wouldn't listen to me. He told me the bridge was named Jeff

Davis and that the old Trinity could not carry enough water to wash "Jeff" out.

About 4 o'clock in the morning, one of Uncle Joe's partners woke us up. "The bridge is gone—not a stick left and the water will soon be up to the house."

Men were stationed on the bridge with long poles to keep logs from striking the piers. A large spruce tree came down the river with roots, branches and all.

The men, seeing it come, and knowing the bridge was doomed, escaped before the roots of the tree struck.

When the tree struck the bridge, it went down as if nothing had been in its way. As the river continued to rise, it began to wash the black loam of the orchard away.

Finally, as the current became stronger, one after the other the fruit trees began to fall.

When the river reached its highest, one could see floating down parts of mills, sluice boxes, miners' cabins, water wheels, hen coops, parts of bridges and bales of hay.

For a distance of one hundred and fifty miles, everything was swept to destruction.

Joe Carr wrote that he was a passenger on the old steamer, *Gem*, traveling from Sacramento to Red Bluff.

> *The only way the pilot could tell where the channel of the river was, was by the cottonwood trees on each side of the river. The boat stopped several times to take men out of the tops of trees and off the roofs of houses.*

The city of Sacramento suffered the worst damage because off its levee, which lay in a wide and flat valley at the junction of the American and Sacramento Rivers.

When the floodwaters entered from the higher ground on the East, the levee acted as a dam to keep the water inside the city rather than letting it flow out.

Soon, the water level was 10 feet higher inside than the level of the Sacramento River on the outside of the levee.

A chain gang was sent to break open the levee letting the water escape.

One fur trapper recalled that Sacramento had been hit hard by floods before. He remembered traveling over the area in a row boat. In 1846, he said, the water was seven feet deep for sixty days.

Sacramento was hit by floods in 1849, in 1850, in 1851, and twice in the winters of 1852 and 1853.

It was at this time that Sacramento businessmen decided to do something about the flooding. In the summer of 1853, the business part of Sacramento was raised four feet by filling the streets with dirt, and then a levee or bank of earth was built about the town.

Not less than forty-five Chinese men were carried away in their cabins at Oregon Bar in Placer County. It has now been determined that many more, as many as one thousand, stayed in their cabins and perished.

The American River rose 55 feet. It is said that the rich men lost a large portion of their property during the flood. The poor lost all.

Sacramento in 1862 flood.

Sacramento waterfront in 1862.

A 1954 flood isolated the house of Manual Seamus in the pocket area of Sacramento.

Chapter 5

Lady Adams Building

The Lady Adams Building at 119 K Street in Old Sacramento.

T he Lady Adams dates back to 1852, when two German merchants built it as a wholesale and import house. It was named after the ship, *Lady Adams*. Many of the materials in the building came from the ship itself, including the brick that was used as ballast.

The crusty old Lady Adams vessel brought the German merchants around the horn to Old Sacramento.

In a fire in 1852, when nearly every single structure in Old Sacramento was reduced to ashes, The Lady Adams building miraculously remained undamaged. Its protection from the fire that swept Old Sacramento is believed to have been its brick roof.

The building was erected in 1852 by the Lady Adams Mercantile Company at a cost of $29,000. The building was named for the brig that brought the partners around the horn.

The first owners of the Lady Adams were the German merchants whose names seem to have been lost to history. After setting up their business in a tent, the German merchants had the Lady Adams built.

The mast of the Lady Adams was used as a "backing-up" stop for wagons.

In the 1950s, Old Sacramento went through its "skid row" days and the Lady Adams was a flop house, as well as a brothel. It then became vacant and fell into disrepair.

In 1970, the brick roof that saved the building from the 1852 fire, collapsed and caused serious damage to the building.

The Lady Adams was restored and is now used as a retail building in Old Sacramento.

Chapter 6

The Cholera Epidemic

NOTICE.

PREVENTIVES OF

CHOLERA!

Published by order of the Sanatory Committee, under the sanction of the Medical Council.

BE TEMPERATE IN EATING & DRINKING!
Avoid Raw Vegetables and Unripe Fruit!
Abstain from COLD WATER, when heated, and above all from *Ardent Spirits*, and if habit have rendered them indispensable, take much less than usual.

SLEEP AND CLOTHE WARM !
☞DO NOT SLEEP OR SIT IN A DRAUGHT OF AIR.
Avoid getting Wet !
Attend immediately to all disorders of the Bowels.
TAKE NO MEDICINE WITHOUT ADVICE.

Medicine and Medical Advice can be had by the poor, at all hours of the day and night, by applying at the Station House in each Ward.

CALEB S. WOODHULL, *Mayor*
JAMES KELLY, *Chairman of Sanitary Committee.*

The year was 1850. A man disembarked from the *New World* ship, stepped onto the levee in Sacramento, and died.

He was the first of 1,000 deaths to follow from the most devastating cholera epidemic in the western United States.

Asiatic cholera is a bacterium spread by a contaminated water supply and passed from person to person. The disease spread like a wildfire through the garbage-strewn streets of Sacramento.

Victims began suffering abdominal cramps, diarrhea, vomiting and dehydration. Their eyes shrank into their heads and death followed within hours.

Panic developed. Families abandoned their relatives. Some hid the dead relatives and those not buried were thrown into the water.

Doctors John Morse and Thomas Logan worked tirelessly. Seventeen doctors died in the process of caring for the victims.

Dr. Pete Ahrens wrote extensively about cholera and its causes.

"Cholera reached California simultaneously by sea and land. The overland route to Sacramento was strewn with the corpses of pioneers and native people known and unknown."

Sacramento's provisional government was without resources to do more than furnish coffins for the stricken. J.D.B. Stillman, personal physician to Leland Stanford, said he counted one thousand graves in the vicinity of Sacramento, "...over which the grass had not yet grown."

Without exception, victims of the cholera disease were buried in mass graves. There were several such graves, the largest being at New Helvetia cemetery.

Dr. Stillman wrote, "The chronic disease of California may have masked the precise moment of the arrival by land of Asiatic cholera in Sacramento. Crossroads and port cities were vulnerable with every new traveler."

The Sacramento *Transcript* carried a headline about the news that "Twenty-two cases of cholera and thirteen deaths" arrived on the *Carolina* in San Francisco October 9, 1850.

The report erroneously said, "The cholera had entirely disappeared from on board a few days prior to the steamer's arrival at San Francisco. She was not quarantined."

Dr. John Morse, one of the doctors attending the sick in the 1850 epidemic, believed the disease arrived with a "steerage immigrant". The immigrant was found collapsed on the Sacramento levee beyond help.

Sacramento's city council passed an ordinance requiring owners or occupants of property to cleanse all filth and rubbish within 24 hours or be hit with a $500 fine.

The Sacramento *Transcript* duly noted the response to the order. "The bonfires from Third and Eighth streets to J gave the appearance of a general conflagration."

Advertisements began to appear in newspapers, promising cures for the cholera disease. One such ad said, "No one should be without a bottle of it in his pocket, in case of any sudden attack."

Dr. James Blake, a physician at the cholera hospital in St. Louis, wrote, "The experience I had as physician to the Cholera Hospital led me to the conclusion that the indiscriminate use of these cholera specifics is as fatal as the epidemic itself."

Sacramento offered a prime location for the cholera disease. Its location was in a low-lying alluvial soil near a river. Sacramento was said to be more prone to cholera because the disease's best means of local dissemination was through an infected water supply.

Cholera first struck Sacramento while it was awaiting the news of California's admission to the Union.

The epidemic reached its peak on October 31. Fifty deaths were reported for that day by the *Transcript*. Of these, 36 were said to be from cholera.

Hospitals were ill-prepared to handle the cholera epidemic. Dr. J.M. Mackenzie, a member of the Common Council, said the city hospital was so crowded that those applying for admission were in such destitute condition the only way of guarding against vermin was a new supply of clothing. The hospital had no such clothing supply.

In a Grand Jury investigation, it was found that the city hospital was in deplorable condition. One of the main wards had 50 patients. Some patients had no sheets, some had one, some had two, and those who had sheets had not had them changed for eight to 21 days.

After the peak of the epidemic was reached on October 31, the death rate proceeded downward with fluctuations. A newspaper reporter wrote "The disease is certainly on the wane...no deaths have occurred this morning."

The epidemic was soon forgotten.

Business became the order of the day in Sacramento. Miners bought supplies, preparing for the winter.

The Settlers and Miners Tribune wrote, "The strong and active that have fallen within the past few weeks are apparently forgotten and their places filled by others."

The term cholera has been applied in various combinations since Hippocrates to a set of symptoms presented by virulent gastro-enteric maladies.

In 1817, a lethal series of world cholera pandemics began, according to Dr. Pete Ahrens. The disease emanated from the Bengal in eastern India to follow the tracks of armies and maritime traffic.

The first pandemic affected the wide region of the southern Eurasian continent, circulating from China westward through Afghanistan to Arabia, into east Africa and southward to Zanzibar.

At Mecca, in 1831, cholera broke out among pilgrims, killing half of them for about 12,000 deaths.

Chapter 7

California Hunts
For A Capitol Site

State Capitol finally finds a home.

Historians don't agree on where California's first state capitol was. Some claim it was San Jose, while others insist it was Monterey.

Let's see if we can shed some light on this delicate matter. Because of its accessible Port, Monterey was named the Capital of Spanish California in 1776. That same year, Juan Bautista de Anza arrived in California with the first Spanish settlers.

In 1822, Mexico won its independence from Spain. It acquired the land that is now California in the settlement process. Monterey then became the Mexican capital and California pledged its allegiance to Mexico.

Then, the United States won the battle with Mexico in the Mexican-American War. Under the Treaty of Guadalupe Hidalgo, Alta California and New Mexico became United States territories.

This two-story building was California's first state capitol building.

At that time, Monterey was still the capital of *Alta California*.

In 1846, Commodore John Drake Sloat arrived in Monterey Bay and raised the American flag, claiming it for California. Mexico gave up California without a fight.

Delegates from around California met in Monterey in 1849 to create a constitution for the new state of California. The delegates decided against keeping Monterey as the state's capital.

A two-story adobe hotel measuring 60 feet by 40 feet was selected as the first capitol build in San Jose. The top floor was for the Assembly and the bottom floor was for the Senate.

Legislative members soon began to grumble over their choice for a capitol site. Offers poured in from other communities offering land and accommodations if the legislature would only select them as the site of the state's capitol building.

One of the most promising offers came from General Mariano Vallejo. His offer was accepted and the state's legislature voted to move the state's headquarters to Vallejo.

Vallejo has twice served as the capital of the state of California. Once in 1852, and then again in 1853. Both periods were very brief in tenure.

When the legislature convened for its third session, the Vallejo capitol building was not ready. Workmen were still completing the buildings. Not only was the furniture and fixtures not in place, most of it had not even arrived.

The steamer *Empire* housed about 250 people. Fifty of these were legislators. The steamer's facilities were considered inadequate for legislative purposes. The legislators deemed its contract with General Vallejo to be in default.

A compromise was reached to avoid further tensions. The legislators agreed to keep the capital in Vallejo but continue its current session in Sacramento.

The next year, when the legislature met for its fourth session, building conditions had improved but the weather hadn't. Roads were difficult to navigate. When Benicia offered the legislators the free use of its city hall and port of call on the river, it was accepted.

The session was continued with little complaint until it adjourned in May 1853.

When the fifth session of the legislature convened in 1854, it found it had 100 men with no place to sleep except in saloons. Again, the legislators began talking of change.

Sacramento made a generous offer of its Sacramento County Courthouse as a meeting site. It had many additional rooms, plus a fireproof vault and free moving for all legislators.

Sacramento also offered a free building site for a new capitol building. The legislators accepted the offer and the same day, all the belongings of the legislators, governor and staff was loaded onto the steamer *Wilson G. Hunt* for the trip to Sacramento.

Legislators found their new site in Sacramento had what they needed. The two-story building supported a balcony, and the town had all forms of transportation, from buggies to steamboat service.

There were plenty of facilities to house all of the legislative people. Unfortunately, a fire destroyed the courthouse right after the legislature ended its session.

A new building was completed by January 1855. The front of the building had eight large fluted pillars. The second floor was 80 by 120 feet and provided room for the senate and the assembly, plus other necessary offices. The ground floor provided offices, plus it had fireproof vaults for the state's treasury.

The public square, bordered by Ninth and Tenth streets on two sides, and by I and J streets on the other two, was donated by the city for the new state capitol building.

When the great flood of 1861-62 racked Sacramento, the legislature moved its operations to San Francisco on a temporary basis.

The legislature conducted its business in the Merchants Exchange Building at Battery and Washington streets. They were able to return to Sacramento when the next session began.

It took 14 years to construct the new state capital that was designed by M.F. Butler. Special taxes had to be levied to keep the project going.

As delays occurred, other cities renewed their bids to become the state capital, but none were successful.

The legislature was able to move into the new building on November 26, 1869, the Governor and Secretary of State and his staff took up residence in the new building.

The legislature convened in its new building December 6, 1869. Work on the building continued until it was completed in 1874.

Chapter 8

The Round Tent Saloon And the Eagle Theater

The Eagle Theater

Zadock Hubbard was so elated with the success of his Round Tent Saloon he decided to add a theater.

At the Round Tent Saloon, the usual price for a drink was a pinch of gold dust. This was an arbitrary amount, depending on the size of the bartender's fingers.

The Round Tent Saloon was built on the corner of Embarcadero (Front and J streets) in the late spring of 1849 by Hubbard and his partners Gates Brown and Madison Pruett.

The saloon was not only successful as a waterhole for the gold miners, but was a prime location to exchange gold dust and nuggets for U.S. coins. Paper money was not popular at the time. It was perceived to have less value than hard metal coins and was prone to destruction by fire.

The original Eagle Theater playhouse was built of wood frame and canvas, with a tin roof. It was open for only three months when it was destroyed by fire.

The Eagle Theater first opened to a full house in July 1849 with a production of "The Bandit Chief", or "The Spectre of the Forest." Spectators wore heavy overcoats, felt hats, and knee high boots.

It's estimated the original cost of the Eagle Theater was $30,000. Historical accounts say the original theater was 30 feet wide.

The *Placer Times* had this to say about the theater's opening offering:

>*This house opened on Thursday evening to a full and we may add, fashionable house, for the 'dress circle' was graced by quite a number of fine looking well-costumed ladies, the sight of whom was somewhat revivifying.*
>
>*Of the performances, we have no room to speak in detail, nor to point out many imperfections, which no doubt will be corrected after a few representations.*

*Messrs. Hubbard, Brown & Co.,
deserve the patronage of the theater-
going public for building such a
comfortable and well-arranged house.*

Seats in the theater were rough boards, apparently without seat backs and possibly sitting on tree stumps or packing crates.

General lighting was provided by three multi-candle chandeliers, while stage lighting was achieved with oil lamps placed directly in front of the stage.

The Placer Times said the orchestra consisted of a violin, a large drum, and an iron triangle that did double duty in announcing meals at a nearby boarding house. The paper added that "a very cheesy flageolet" (a small flute) was tootled by a one-eyed musician.

The theater venture ended in calamity for Zadock Hubbard who over-extended himself in its construction. He became ill to the point that his sanity became in doubt.

He was forced to sell to his partners to stave off creditors. Gates Brown and Madison Pruett were forced to sell the property for $4,350. After minor repairs the Eagle Theater reopened with the popular tragedy "Douglas".

The theater's final curtain was drawn by the 1850 floods, breaking up a performance in midpoint.

The drunken audience ignored the flood waters, even gambling on the wooden benches between acts. Sometimes a rowdy miner would fling out his arms, striking customers on each side of him, knocking them in the water.

Everybody thought it was hilarious except for those poor soles that were dunked in the water.

The water kept rising and the play came to an end. The Eagle Theater lost all its costumes and scenery.

The flood-damaged theater was purchased by McDougall, Fowler and Warbass, and shifted 200 feet east, so that it faced Second Street between I and J streets.

Chapter 9

Sacramento River's Steamships

The Delta Queen

Paddlewheeler steamships plied the Sacramento River for 100 years, churning their way through the Delta waters. The steamboat captains were adventurous characters who often took their vessels into uncharted waters.

The side wheeler Carrie Ladd

If another boat challenged a captain to a race, he might respond without regard to his passengers. He turned up the boilers.

At Sacramento, passengers bound for San Francisco debarked from trains and stepped across a levee to the waiting steamships. Some of the steamships were described as floating palaces.

The upper saloon might resemble a large hall in an English country home. The dining room was located on the lower part of the vessel. At night, gas jets were used to make the dining room a well-lit experience.

Before 1847, it was John Sutter's own schooner, the *Sacramento*, that made the trips between Sacramento and Yerba Buena (San Francisco) Sutter purchased the craft from the Russians at Fort Ross. The Sacramento was the fastest boat on the river.

In his book, *Sacramento, Excursions into Its History*, William M. Holden reported that Sutter's schooner was so overloaded with wheat that it

54

spilled over the coamings (raised pieces of wood or iron around the hatch coverings).

The Wilson B. Hunt

The *Sacramento* was skippered by John Yates, who was not known for his sobriety. Kanaka sailors formed the crew on the *Sacramento*.

Another Russian built boat on the Sacramento River was the *Sitka*. It was the first steam-powered ship on the river. The 37-foot side-wheeler was brought to Sacramento by William Leidesdorff.

The boat was disassembled in Alaska after Leidesdorff bought it sight-unseen. It was carried to San Francisco Bay on a bark and reassembled for the trip to Sacramento.

In San Francisco, it was raised and the engine removed, converting it to the schooner *Rainbow*.

One estimate placed the number of paddle wheelers on the Sacramento River at 300.

The *Delta Queen* and her sister the *Delta King* were launched in Stockton in 1927 at the time when the heyday of steam boating was about over.

The two boats never operated successfully from a financial standpoint. Their primary runs were between Sacramento and San Francisco, one coming and one going.

The two steamers were pressed into military service during World War II, serving as billets and to transport troops around the Bay area.

The *Delta King*, engineless and sunk, was rescued by Sacramento entrepreneurs and restored to become a popular dockside restaurant in old Sacramento.

The *Lady Washington* was brought to Sutter's Embarcadero on a sailing ship. It was reassembled in Sacramento. She thrashed her way up the American River to Coloma, only to be snagged and sunk on her return voyage.

The grand 226-foot side wheeler *Senator* arrived in 1849, taking more than seven months to make the trip from her home port of New York.

The *Senator* was a familiar sight for more than 30 years as it made its San Francisco to Sacramento run. It took time out now and then to make a run down the coast to San Diego.

The boating glut soon became obvious. Both Stockton and Sacramento had more steamboat passenger capacity than it did passengers. Fierce price wars occurred.

At one time the price of passage dropped as low as 25 cents rather than the $30 charged by the Senator.

The *John A. Sutter* that ran so profitably from Stockton to Marysville exploded in June 1850. The boat became a total wreck.

In 1851, the steamer *Sagamore* had a boiler explosion as it was departing from the wharf in San Francisco, killing 50 persons.

One of the Delta's most loved steamers was the *Yosemite*. The 248 foot vessel pulled away from the docks at Rio Vista one evening when her boilers exploded, killing 45 people.

As settlements grew along the Delta waterways, steamboats became a dependable means of transportation. Better boilers were also being made. People developed favorites among the steamers and side-wheelers.

Stocktonians loved the *T.C. Walker* and the *J.D. Peters*. Isleton folks were smitten with the *Isleton* and *Pride of the River*. Sacramentans thought the *Chrissie* and the 245-foot *Chrysopolis* were the classiest.

The *Chrysopolis* set a new record of five hours and 19 minutes for the run from Sacramento to San Francisco. It could carry 1,000 passengers.

For sheer nerve, no captain could beat the bravado of Captain Ned Wakeman, of the *New World*. While this 220-foot side-wheeler was still on the the ways at New York Harbor, the sheriff seized her because of a creditor's lien.

Through chicanery and force of an armed crew, Captain Wakeman had the boat launched with the steam up and a full load of coal on board. He headed for San Francisco by the only route possible, around the Horn.

In Rio de Janeiro, a yellow fever epidemic was encountered, killing 20 of his crew (24,000 people in Rio de Janeiro died).

The *New World* was fired upon by a British frigate and by Brazilian army forces wanting to confiscate the vessel.

Captain Wakeman guided the *New World* into the Golden Gate with 250 cash-paying passengers, enough to pay off creditors. Wakeman then set a new record for the Sacramento to San Francisco run that held up for more than a decade.

There were other smaller paddle wheelers that carried passengers up the smaller rivers and sloughs, often in water so shallow the passengers were obliged to take a shovel and dig the boats off of sandbars of mudbars.

They went up the Tuolumne and Stanislaus rivers, and up the American, Feather and Yuba. They parted the tules at French Camp Slough and went into the South Delta to Old River.

The little steamer *Pert* was the first to make it up the Mokuelumnes to the fledgling settlement of Woodbridge. These runs were just too perilous to become established trips.

Chapter 10

Boomtown

Front Street in Sacramento in 1850.

Sacramento flourished as the gold miners rushed in to make their fortunes. In mid-June 1849, Sacramento had 100 wood and canvas houses. Two months later, it had 1,000.

Prospector William L. Schooning eye-witnessed the unbridled growth taking place. "Yesterday we drove our teams into the streets about 9 o'clock in the morning. We let the team stand there for about two hours. In the evening of the same day, I passed along the very ground where the horses had been, and a baker's shop was in full operation."

The real city of Sacramento started around a wharf called the Embarcadero at the junction where the Sacramento and American rivers meet. The port was used by gold miners heading out for the gold fields.

Businessmen Sam Brannan, Peter Burnett (later a governor of California) and George McDougall, (brother of future governor John McDougall), were attracted to the waterfront location.

John Sutter, Jr., was now in charge of his father's affairs. He and McDougall disagreed over terms of the lease of the location. A trade war erupted between Sutter's Sacramento City and McDougall's new base of operations at Sutterville. Sutterville was built by John Sutter, Sr. who opposed many of his son's decisions.

Sacramento did not have gambling houses and saloons until the summer of 1849. Neither did the new city have a formal government.

Gambling institutions in the regions liked the "alcalde" form of government. It was inevitable, the gambling houses and the saloon trade won. Sacramento became a boomtown.

Sacramento petitioned the legislature to drop the "City" from its name, becoming "Sacramento", which the legislature approved.

Hardin Bigelow became Sacramento's first mayor. He spurred forth efforts to protect the city from future disasters, such as the flood of 1850 when the Sacramento and American rivers crested simultaneously.

In that storm, merchandize at the Embarcadero was not secured and washed away in the flood. Bigelow stood strongly behind the building of dams and levees to protect the city.

After the city experienced its first fire, in which a number of businesses were destroyed, citizen volunteers formed California's first fire protection program, called the Mutual Hook and Ladder Company.

Sacramento Mutual Hook and Ladder Company

The city adapted iron window shutters to reduce wind draft and make fires harder to spread.

At this same time, the *New World* steamship brought news that California had been admitted to the Union. The same ship also brought a cholera epidemic that killed from 800 to 1,000 people over three and a half weeks.

New arrivals refused to honor John Sutter's title to so much land. Squatters who wanted to take Sutter's land grant holdings worked to find loopholes in the law.

Sutter's empire began to disintegrate when he decided to back the unpopular Alta California governor Manuel Micheltorena. Micheltorena was overthrown by Alvarado and Jose Castro in 1841.

Sacramento's waterfront was known as Sutter's Embarcadero.

The push for recognition of squatter's rights led to the formation of a Law and Order Association among the squatters. Sacramentans also founded the Vigilance Committee, patterned after a similar committee in San Francisco.

After lynching a prisoner, the committee dissolved when it lost support by demanding that the mayor step down for interfering. The mayor refused to step down and the committee was ended.

By 1849, a number of log cabins and frame buildings were erected on the waterfront. The town grew so rapidly that the population rose to more than 6,000 people, 4,000 of whom were transients.

Daniel B. Woods, who arrived in Sacramento in June 1849, noted that each "hot flash" of new discovery in the hills triggered an exodus from Sacramento.

Sutter's New Helvetia collapsed completely in 1852. Sutter's fort was abandoned and Sacramento's commerce became reliant on coins. The city had outgrown its unstable gold rush.

That same year 1852 saw Sacramento grow in a new direction. Pharmacies, attorney firms, brass foundries, and lingerie shops opened along the streets of Sacramento. The Embarcadero no longer determined the growth of Sacramento.

Chapter 11

The Sacramento Valley Railroad

The Sacramento Valley Railroad was the first railroad west of the Mississippi.

Getting mail and supplies to Sacramento was a major undertaking. It was either brought over the Sierra by wagon or hauled around the Horn by ship.

Charles Lincoln Wilson (he founded the town of Lincoln) saw an opportunity for a railroad service.

A group of businessmen earlier incorporated the Sacramento, Auburn and Nevada Railroad. Their plans fell through when they found it would costs two million dollars to lay the first section of track.

Charles Lincoln Wilson

Wilson reorganized the abandoned railroad company and formed the Sacramento Valley Railroad in August 1852. Wilson went to New York to gather talent to build the railroad.

There, he met Theodore Judah, whom he brought to California in 1854 to survey the railroad. Judah designed a route that ran down R Street in Sacramento and along present-day Folsom Boulevard and across the river to Negro Bar.

The original plan was to run the line all the way to Marysville by way of Folsom. These plans never fully materialized as the railroad was only built as far as Folsom.

Theodore Judah, designer of the Sacramento Valley Railroad.

The Sacramento Valley Railroad ran from the Sacramento River levee at Front and L Street in Old Sacramento and terminated at Folsom.

The first train operated over the 22.9-mile line on February 22, 1856.

The Sacramento Valley Railroad was consolidated with the Folsom and Placerville Railroad to form the Sacramento and Placerville Railroad.

The Sacramento Valley Railroad carried the Pony Express mail between Sacramento and Folsom, a distance of 22 miles. Folsom was the terminus of the Pony Express riders from June 1860 to 1861, when the western terminus became Placerville.

A photo of the Placerville and Sacramento County rail line.

Charles Lincoln Wilson successfully lobbied the State Legislature to allow construction of a railroad between Sacramento and Marysville. The route would head 22 miles east to Negro Bar, which later became Folsom. It would cross the American River and skirt along the foothills for 20 miles north to Marysville.

Judah's major obstacles in designing the railroad were the building of railroad trestles over three creeks and cutting a 600-foot-long embankment near Negro Bar.

To cut expenses in building the railroad, the labor force was reduced from 150 to 90. Many of the laborers were Chinese workers. Charles Crocker adopted Wilson's idea of using Chinese workers when the Big Four Built the Intercontinental Railroad.

The Sacramento Valley Railroad led directly to the building of the transcontinental railroad. As a result of the 22-miles of track to Folsom, laws were passed that eased railroad financing.

Judah came to California, eager to find a path for the tracks of a railroad over the Sierra.

The initial run of the Sacramento Valley Railroad was a major event. The locomotive broke down just short of Folsom. To keep passengers happy, they arrived safely in Folsom and was treated to a party that lasted into the next morning.

Chapter 12

The Governor's Mansion

The Governor's Mansion

The State of California bought the Governor's Mansion in 1903 for $32,500. The house was originally built for Albert and Clemenza Gallatin. He was a partner in the Sacramento hardware store of Huntington and Hopkins.

The mansion is located at the corner of 16th and H streets. Gallatin hired architect Nathaniel Goodell to build the house.

The salon in the Governor's Mansion.

Governor George Pardee and his family were the first residents of the "new" Governor's Mansion. It was home to 12 other governors during the next 64 years.

In the handcrafted bronze hinges on the inner hallway doors, a hummingbird has been molded in the center of each of the matching door knobs. Mr. Gallatin is said to have paid 25 cents each for the hummingbirds, wholesale.

To make the raised design ceilings, plaster was pushed through a cone onto a glazed paper lying on a cool surface. After the designs hardened, glue was applied and they were hand-held against the ceiling until the glue dried.

When the designs were attached, gold leaf was applied to the raised designs.

The furniture in the parlor was selected by Mrs. Earl Warren in the 1940s. Although the purchase price for all of the rugs in the parlor was approximately $10,000, they are considered worth many times that amount today.

The breakfast room in the Governor's Mansion

The main salon in the Governor's Mansion

Chapter 13

The Second Governor's Mansion

Mansion constructed for Reagan in 1970. The Reagan's never lived in it.

When Ronald Reagan was elected Governor of California he and his wife Nancy lived in the old Governor's Mansion at 15th and H streets. Their stay there lasted three months.

Nancy was sure it was a fire trap and wanted out of there. This made Reagan the last governor to have ever lived in the Governor's Mansion.

The state of California then built a new Governor's Mansion in 1970, located 10 miles from downtown Sacramento. This wasn't completed during Reagan's governorship.

Then the obstinate Jerry Brown called it a Taj Majal and refused to live there. He chose instead to rent an apartment where he could place his mattress on the floor to match his Bohemian style.

After sitting idle for months and months, the state of California decided to put the house on the market. It held a first auction, but received no bids that were high enough.

In a second auction, southern California developer Matt Franich submitted the highest bid. The State declared his bid didn't arrive on time. Franich insisted it did.

The state did some rechecking and found Franich's lost bid. Fearing a lawsuit, the state rejected all bids and held a third auction. This time Franich won with a bid of $1,550,000.

Franich then received a subpoena from an attorney representing one of the donors who contributed to the effort to purchase the property in the first place. The donor said the state had no right to sell it to Franich.

It took nearly a year to close escrow. Franich said he was told the state had worked out an agreement with the donors, allowing it to sell the property, but wouldn't tell him the details.

When we first looked at the property, Franich said, the grounds were nice and green. Before we closed escrow, Franich said, he suggested the state allow him to go in with his own people and maintain the property.

The state refused. At the close of escrow, the mansion and grounds were in bad shape. "Trees were dying and the grass was dead."

The confusion doesn't end there.

"When they handed us the keys, we couldn't get in," said Franich.

The state hadn't finished the construction. The house was a shell with little or no lighting. The floors weren't in. They were basically concrete, with some tile.

Franich described the estate further, "The grounds had no walls, no gates, no landscaping. The fence was chain link, with a chicken-coop gate.

"At the first rain, the Governor's office and library and formal dining room were inundated. The state of the art solar system was leaking like a sieve, and never did work."

Franich's torment didn't end there. Expanding ice in the solar system broke all its parts. The State architect said it would cost $35,000 to replace them.

"The roof was leaking badly. There were two inches of water in the living room on the first rain.

"The caretaker was manufacturing furniture here. His wife was canning and processing food for sale. Two catering companies worked out of here. About 15 people listed this address as their residence."

Franich said he moved 350 cubic yards of garbage that had been dumped there.

Still Franich was in love with the place. It had awesome dimensions, he said. "The main roof beam, a whopper 220 feet long and almost six feet deep, costs $148,000 in 1974, more than most houses cost today."

Franich launched improvements galore. He installed 11,000 floor tiles, and laid down 40 Persian rugs. He planted more than 200 trees, erected an adobe-type fence with wrought-iron gates.

He installed 607 outdoor security lights and closed circuit television monitors. He added a 50 by 30 foot swimming pool with fountains, a spa with lion's head fountains flanking a waterfall, and an opulent bathhouse and sauna.

The mansion has 10 bedrooms, 11 bathrooms, two kitchens, three dining rooms, and a total of 31 rooms.

"I spent more money to restore it than it cost to build," Franich said.

Franich planted more than 400 trees, including peaches, nectarines, cherries, avocados and persimmons. They bought antiques and furniture from around the world, including three chandeliers from Italy for the formal dining room.

A huge 60-inch diameter chandelier with hand-cut crystals from Austria went into the ballroom.

The mansion's Old Sacramento Room has a bar where Black Bart slaked his thirst in Jackson. The bar was salvaged when the Jackson Hotel was razed.

When Governor Deukmejian was elected Governor, he balked at the state paying $18,000 a month rent that Franich was asking for a building the state had just sold.

Deukmejian turned thumbs down on the deal and moved into a $400,000 home purchased with contributor money.

The Franich's have hosted as many as 1,100 people at one time at the mansion and raised $1 million for charities.

Franich got another jolt in 1984. He learned there was an Indian burial ground on the property, a point the state failed to disclose.

"This house was built to demonstrate the power and stature of a California Governor. "There'll be a Governor here someday."

Chapter 14

Crocker Art Museum

The Crocker Art Museum

The Crocker Art Museum doesn't just have visual art. It plays host to music, dinner events, live shows, theater, sing-alongs and camps/classes.

The Crocker Art Museum is one of the longest continuously operating museums in the west. It is located in Sacramento at 216 O Street.

It started out as a private collection of Edwin and Margaret Crocker. Their mansion and their art works was donated to the city of Sacramento in 1885.

Crocker Museum is renowned for its California art, but it also has a large Asian section, and items from Africa, Oceania and some Greek paintings.

In 1869, Edwin B. Crocker and his wife Margaret began to assemble a significant collection of paintings and drawings during an extended trip to Europe.

Edward B. Crocker

Crocker was a Supreme Court Justice. He first earned a degree in civil engineering in New York. He went on to study law in Indiana. Upon his second marriage to Margaret Rhodes, the couple moved to Sacramento.

In Sacramento, he resumed his legal career and became active in politics. He was chairman of the Republican Party. In 1863, Governor Leland Stanford appointed him Justice of the Supreme Court.

Charles Christian Nahl's 1872 painting, "Sunday Morning in the Mines.

Crocker, in 1864, became legal counsel for the Central Pacific Railroad. He was a brother of Charles Crocker, one of the Big Four that developed the Railroad Line.

Work caused a stress on Parker. He suffered a stroke in 1869 and retired to take up less stressful hobbies.

The Crocker Museum boasts it has 150 years of painting, sculpture, and craft media covering genres that include Impressionism, Abstract

Expressionism, and Pop Art. It features artists such as Thomas Hill, Guy Rose, Joan Brown and Wayne Thiebaud.

In 1868, Judge Crocker purchased the property and existing buildings on the corner of Third and O Street. He commissioned Seth Babson, a local architect, to redesign and renovate the home into a grander, Italianate mansion.

In addition, Crocker asked Babson to design an elaborate gallery building that would sit adjacent to the mansion and display the family's growing art collection.

The controversial expansion tripled the Crocker's size to 145,000 square feet. It added four times the space for traveling exhibitions and three times the space for the Museum to showcase it permanent collection.

Chapter 15

Old City Cemetery

Sacramento Historic City Cemetery

A requirement to be buried here is you must be dead. Sacramento Historic City Cemetery is a grand place to explore history. It's also a good place to talk with old friends.

Some of the tombstones themselves spark a smile in most visitors. Take this one which stands watch over Robert Samuel Spear, who died in 1971 at the young age of 17.

The epitaph is simple, but so real. It says:

"See you later".

There are more than 35,000 people buried in the Old City Cemetery at 10th and Broadway. If living, they would fill a good-sized town.

The people buried there came from the hordes of immigrants that funneled into Sacramento from all over the globe to find their fortunes in the Gold Rush. Few did, but others found success in other ways, some became entrepreneurs.

If you listen closely to the docents at the cemetery, you'll probably hear one quip, "People are dying to get in here." The docents know their job. It's almost as though they are trying to bring the city's cemeteries back to life.

It's a lively place indeed. It's not only adorned by beautiful statues and dramatic markers, but it's a lush flower garden as well. It contains some well-known people.

The people buried there go back to 1849, when the cemetery was established. Walk the walk and you find where mayors, California governors, Civil War veterans, Volunteer Firemen and victims of the 1850 Cholera epidemic are buried.

The City Cemetery is the oldest existing cemetery in Sacramento. It was designed to resemble a Victorian garden. Pathways and grand avenues wander through the 31-acre cemetery.

The cemetery has a historic Gold Rush era Rose garden, a perennial plants area and several acres of native plants. Helping the Old City Cemetery

Committee maintain the intensive care areas are 100 plus volunteers.

This was part of a time capsule to be opened when it reaches 100 years old.

Curiously, the cemetery's web site notes that all cemetery plots have been sold, but the cemetery continues to have 15-30 burials there each year. These burials are for families that obviously purchased their plots before they died and hold the deeds to the plots.

It may be possible that holders of deeds can sell them to others who might want to purchase them.

The original ground for the cemetery was donated by John Augustus Sutter in 1849. He donated 10 acres to the city to be used as a cemetery.

In 1850, 600 victims of the cholera epidemic were buried in mass graves in City Cemetery. The remainder of the 800 to 1000 victims was buried in the nearby New Helvetia Cemetery, also in mass graves.

In 1856, the city engaged a cemetery superintendent and began to plan the grounds. In 1857, a gatehouse and bell tower were constructed. These were demolished in 1949 during the widening of Broadway.

Several fraternal groups purchased sections for their members, including the Masons, Odd Fellows, and the Sacramento Pioneers Association. There is another section set aside for volunteer firemen in 1858 and members of the Grand Army of the Republic in 1878.

The City of Sacramento owns the cemetery, which encompasses 44 acres. In 1986, a group of residents became concerned by the lack of maintenance and ongoing vandalism.

They formed the Old City Cemetery Committee. The Committee later became a part of the Sacramento County Historical Society. In 2003, it became an independent organization dedicated to the preservation of the historic site.

Chapter 16

The Squatter's Riot

The Squatter's Riot was an uprising that took place between squatting settlers and the government of Sacramento. It happened in 1850.

A problem had been brewing since October 1849 when it became apparent that lots close to the river were extremely valuable. Many were vacant and immigrants who arrived later wanted to occupy them at little or no cost, despite the fact that others had paid for them.

The squatters based their claim on a mistake made by the surveyor, Jean Jacques Vioget, who prepared the map which John Sutter used to get his grant in 1841.

The unlikely leader of the "Squatter's Riot" was a brash young man who once walked 40 miles to get help with his eye problem. His name was Charles L. Robinson.

Before entering Amherst College, Robinson walked to Keene, New Hampshire, to see an eye specialist. After getting his eye problems alleviated, he went on to study medicine.

Dr. Charles L. Robinson

In Sacramento, when courts began to take legal action against squatters, Dr. Robinson became involved in organizing the "Squatter's Riot". He and Joseph Maloney challenged Sacramento Mayor Hardin Bigelow and Sheriff Joseph McKinney.

Sacramento Mayor Hardin Bigelow

Settlers arriving in California found that unclaimed land was hard to find and to possess. Out of 14 million acres of land in California, only eight hundred people owned the deeds to differing quantities of land.

Squatters in 1850 Gold Rush

New arrivals who could not afford lodging in Sacramento, squatted on claimed but vacant land around the settlement. Settlers challenged the right of John Sutter's Mexican-era claim to the Sacramento Valley.

The squatters were initially roused by an October 1849 lawsuit against a logger named Z.M. Chapman. Chapman built a log cabin near Sutter's Fort on Priest, Lee & Company owned land.

When Priest, Lee & Company could not produce evidence that they owned the land, Chapman extended his claim. He first challenged the land grants of Sutter and later all city-owned land.

Dr. Charles Robinson jumped into the fray, and sided with Chapman in his actions, building his own shack on another's private land.

The squatting settlers formed the Sacramento Settlers Association.

Sutter's men burned a cabin on the site that Chapman chose to build his cabin. Chapman rebuilt a cabin on the same site. The squatters held a meeting and agreed to retaliate if any more squatter's structures were destroyed.

As the rainy season set in, no further action was taken until spring. In the meantime, Chapman lost his health and returned to the states and didn't renew his claim.

Dr. Charles Robinson, however, continued fighting for the squatter's rights. The Sacramento Settlers Association opened a "recorder's office". It issued certificates of title as follows:

> *We know our rights and, and knowing, dare defend them.*
>
> Office of the Sacramento City Settlers' Association.
>
> *Received of ____fifteen dollars for surveying and recording lot No. ____situated on the ____side of ____street, between ____ and ____street; measuring forty feet front by one hundred and sixty feet in depth, according to the general plan of the city of Sacramento, in conformity with the rules of the association. $15.*
>
> Signed

Surveyor and Register of the
Sacramento Settlers' Association. The
public domain is alike free for all.

Some people purchased lots from Priest, Lee &
Co., a land speculation company. Those that brought
lumber to their lots, had it removed by the squatters
association. The squatters association contended the
lots were illegally bought and sold by Priest, Lee &
Co.

When the lot owners offered a sum of money to
the squatters to desist, the squatters refused.

A petition was submitted to Congress asking for
a distribution of public lands among actual settlers.

Sam Brannan and other land owners spoke up
against Robinson's actions and convinced the
Sacramento City Council to issue a document that
permitted the destruction of Robinson's property.

A major January flood washed through and
destroyed much of Sacramento City, scattering most
of the squatters in the vicinity of city center. This
temporarily dealt with the problem facing the city
council.

Many of the squatters headed north to the placer
mines. When the floods ended and the former
squatters learned there was little gold to be had,
hundreds of them returned to Sacramento City.

Settlers who supported government recognition
of squatter's rights began to host public meetings in
the spring of 1850. They swore to defend their lands
if confronted.

A Law and Order Association was formed and an
irregular militia was organized to challenge the
speculators who charged high prices for the land.

Tension increased when a group of speculators had a squatter-built and squatter-owned fence demolished.

In May 1850, newly-elected Judge E.J. Willis charged a squatter named John T. Madden with unlawful occupation. Squatter-sympathetic settlers charged the speculators with "brute force" in handbills distributed throughout the city.

The squatters rallied behind Dr. Robinson, who worked with *Sacramento Bee* Editor James McClatchy to found the *Settlers and Miners Tribune*.

The *Settlers and Miners Tribune* attacked the land monopoly that stifled new immigration to the city. Robinson enlisted Joseph Maloney to head a company of squatters in case military action was needed.

To keep peace for an additional day, Mayor Hardin Bigelow promised writs for the arrest against those who joined Robinson would not be issued.

However, the next day, such a writ was issued against John T. Madden, who stayed as a squatter prior to his trial. McClatchy and others, who opposed the sheriff's decision to execute the writ, were jailed aboard the *La Grange*, a ship that served as the city's prison.

Maloney and Robinson mobilized a military force. Fearing a full-scale uprising, Mayor Bigelow marched with his fellow settlers and confronted Maloney and Robinson at the corner of 4th and J.

At the downtown confrontation, Bigelow first ordered the squatters to stand down and relinquish their arms. Shooting then began and Bigelow was injured as was Dr. Charles Robinson.

City assessor J.W. Woodland, Joseph Maloney, and a squatter named Jesse Morgan, all died in the fight. Two civilian bystanders were killed in the crossfire.

General Albert Maver Winn, head of the Sacramento City Council at the time, ordered 500 militiamen come to the city. He declared a state of martial law.

The injured Bigelow was unable to continue as mayor. He was replaced by Demas Strong. Charles Robinson, charged with murder, remained extremely popular with the settlers. He was elected to the California State Legislature while still in prison.

The squatter's riot was finally ended, although the federal government upheld Sutter's pre-American grant.

Dr. Charles Robinson was released without standing trial. Robinson returned to Massachusetts where he married his second wife. He then led a party of Free Soilers to Kansas Territory. Robinson became the first governor of Kansas.

The squatters in Sacramento, however, lost their legal battle.

Chapter 17

The Bank of Darius O. Mills

The Bank of Darius O. Mills

Darius Ogden Mills considered investing in gold mining or silver mining as too speculative. Yet it was the gold rush that brought him to Sacramento. Mills came from New York, where he worked as a bank clerk and as a retailer.

Mills founded a bank in 1848. At the time, he was part owner of the Virginia and Truckee

Railroad. This was the link from the Comstock Lode to the Central Pacific Railroad.

William Chapman Ralston

The Bank of California collapsed in the late 1800s, because of financial irregularities involving its chief cashier, William Chapman Ralston.

Ralston lent money to mine owners that would lead to default and repossession. In 1869, Ralston averted a run on the bank by exchanging nearly $1 million worth of gold bars for an equivalent value in gold coin from the U.S. Treasury in San Francisco.

The transaction was carried out in the middle of the night by two of Ralston's associates, Asbury Harpending and Maurice Dore.

William Ogden Mills

When the bank opened in the morning, the sight of tray after tray of gold coin at the tellers' windows quashed any thought by depositors of mounting a run on the bank.

Later, a run on the bank did occur. It was on Thursday, August 26, 1875. The bank failed and Ralston was ruined. The next morning, he turned everything he owned over to William Sharon, an agent of the bank.

Darius Mills used his personal fortune to revive the bank. Along with Sharon, a major investor in the Central Pacific Railroad, the two men were able to attract new investors. Within two years, the bank was strong again.

Mills retired from banking and bought part of Rancho Buri Buri. There he built an estate named Millbrae, the name of the present town on that site.

The 150 acres of the original estate, bordering on San Francisco Bay was leased to Mills' grandson, Ogden L. Mills. It was used for Mills Field, which is now known as San Francisco International Airport.

Chapter 18

Peter H. Burnett

Peter H. Burnett, California's first governor

To say Peter Hardeman Burnett was a controversial character is the largest understatement one could make.

For instance, while serving in Oregon's Provisional Legislature, he proposed and openly advocated preventing African-Americans from moving to Oregon Territory.

Sacramento mining district in 1850.

Blacks who remained in Oregon Territory would be arrested and flogged every six months until they left. He was able to get the Oregon legislature to accept and pass the proposal.

Burnett was born in Nashville, Tennessee and raised in rural Missouri. He received no formal education, but educated himself in law and government.

When gold was discovered in Coloma, Burnett decided to journey south from Oregon and get in on the bonanza. He envisioned a career in law in San Francisco, which was booming.

On his way to the Bay area, he met John Sutter, Jr., who offered Burnett a job selling land plots for the new town of Sacramento. Burnett made nearly $50,000 in land sales in Sacramento.

In 1849, he went to Monterey for the first California Constitutional Convention. On his return to Sacramento, he decided he had enough name recognition to run for the new territory's first civilian governor.

He easily won over four other candidates, including John Sutter. He was sworn in as California's first elected civilian governor December 20, 1849 in San Jose in front of the California State Legislature.

In the first days of his administration, the governor and the California Legislature set out to create the organs of a state government. They created cabinet posts, archives, executive posts and departments, and subdivided the state into 27 counties.

John C. Fremont and William M. Gwin were appointed as state senators. Despite all their preliminary work, the U.S. Congress and President Zachary Taylor had not even recognized California as a U.S. state yet.

Part of this miscommunication was California's remoteness from the federal government. It was also due to over-enthusiastic attitudes by politicians and the public alike to get California into the Union.

California was admitted to the Union as the 31st state by the U.S. Senate on September 9, 1850 as part of the Compromise of 1850. Californians did not learn of their official statehood until one month later.

Governor Burnett's popularity among the State Legislature, the press and the public plummeted. His relations with the legislature began to sour in early 1850, when bills pressing for the incorporation of Sacramento and Los Angeles as city municipalities passed both the State Assembly and the Senate.

Burnett vetoed both bills. He claimed the incorporation bills were unconstitutional and best left to county courts.

The legislature failed to override the Los Angeles incorporation bill, but it did override the Sacramento bill, making Sacramento California's first incorporated city.

Burnett pushed for the exclusion of blacks in California, as he had in Oregon, raising the ire of pro-slavery supporters who wanted to import the Southern slave system to the west coast. He discussed his feelings in his first annual message to the Legislature:

> *For some years past I have given this subject* (African-American settlement in California) *my most serious and candid attention; and I most cheerfully lay before you the result of my own reflections. There is, in my opinion, but one of two consistent courses to take in reference to this class of population; either to admit them to the full and free enjoyment of all the privileges guaranteed by the Constitution to others, or exclude them from the State.*
>
> *If we permit them to settle in our State, under existing circumstances, we consign them, by our own institutions, and the usages of our own society, to a*

subordinate and degraded position, which is in itself but a species of slavery. They would be placed in a situation where they would have not efficient motives for moral or intellectual improvement, but must remain in our midst, sensible of their degradation, unhappy themselves, enemies to the institutions and the society whose usages have placed them there, and for ever fit teachers in all the schools of ignorance, vice and idleness.

We have certainly the right to prevent any class of population from settling in our State, that we may deem injurious to our own society. Had they been born here, and had acquired rights in consequence, I should not recommend any measures to expel. They are not now here, except a few in comparison with the numbers that would be here; and the object is to keep them out.

Burnett also pushed for heavy taxation on foreign immigrants. He signed into law an 1850 Foreign Miners Tax Act requiring every non-American miner to pay $20. He argued for the expansion of capital punishment as well.

With little more than a year in office, Burnett was not only the first governor of California, but he was also the first to resign. Burnett grew frustrated as his agenda ground to a halt.

Burnett became a regular fixture of ridicule and scorn in the state's newspapers and on the floor of the legislature. He cited personal matters for his departure.

Lieutenant Governor John McDougall replaced Burnett on January 9, 1851.

Chapter 19

California's 1st Stagecoach Line

Early-day stagecoach.

James E. Birch was the leading man in bringing the stagecoach to Sacramento. Birch came to California from Providence, Rhode Island in 1849 at the age of 21.

He learned the stagecoach business in New England. He promptly launched a stagecoach business in Sacramento by buying a freight wagon and carrying men to the gold mines.

Birch began to buy out small stage operators in the Central Valley and the gold country. At the end of five years, he had acquired most of the stagecoach lines in California.

He consolidated the lines into the California Stage Company, which he directed from his Sacramento office.

When Wells Fargo achieved a virtual monopoly of the express business in California, it did so not by operating stagecoaches of its own, though it did own a few, but by sending express shipments with stages operated by others.

One of Wells Fargo's chief stagecoach lines was those operated by James Birch.

James Birch was born in South Carolina. Little is known of his early life. It is thought that he grew up in poor circumstances. He first went to New York, and then on to Providence, Rhode Island, where he worked in a livery stable.

He was a stagecoach driver in Providence. At age 21, he decided to join the gold rush crowd, leaving his finance in Massachusetts, where she grew up.

Birch sailed to California on the *SS Crescent City*, arriving there with 100 others on December 23, 1848. When he arrived in Sacramento, he found prices were high. Sacramento was the launching point for the miners heading for the gold fields.

He had his mind made up. He would start a stagecoach business. Initially, his stagecoach was an old ranch wagon Birch bought in the bustling town of Sacramento.

He began hauling passengers from Sacramento City to Coloma in the rugged foothills of the Sierra Nevada. He charged two ounces of gold (about $32 in 1849) for the 50-mile trip, traveling at a rate of 10 to 12 miles per hour.

Birch became adept at forecasting where the next gold panning area would be and was therefore quick to haul gold miners to the new site.

By the middle of 1849, Birch was no longer driving his stagecoaches himself. He left that to his employees while he managed the business. He obtained a fleet of top-of-the-line stagecoaches which he ordered from the east.

Birch's stage line was the envy of all his competitors. Before the end of 1851, Birch was providing stagecoach service to all the northern and southern mining areas east of Stockton.

He returned to Massachusetts in 1852 where he married his fiancée, Julia Chace.

When Birch returned to California, he was making good use of Sacramento's newspapers to build his business. He began selling off the stage lines that operated in areas that were about played out in gold.

He used his profits to add new lines. Facing stern competition, Birch lowered his rates. His California Stage Company began selling shares in the company for $1000 per share. The company was incorporated with a value of $1 million.

He began spending more time in the east with his wife. In 1856, they had a son, Frank Stevens Birch, named after Birch's best friend.

Birch began lobbying certain legislators, such as his friend William M. Gwin, one of California's two senators. Birch wanted to provide U.S. mail service across the Sierra Nevada.

In 1857, Birch was traveling to New York aboard the paddle steamer *SS Central America*. The ship ran into a hurricane and floundered for several days before sinking.

Many passengers managed to reach lifeboats and were rescued. James Birch was not among them.

Chapter 20

The McClatchy Newspaper

James McClatchy

James McClatchy experienced a shipwreck in Baja California before reaching the gold fields in the Sierra Nevada. He tried mining with miserable results.

He then took a job with the *Placer Times*, published at Sutter's Fort. The year was 1849 and McClatchy developed a reputation as a people's champion.

McClatchy took a stand against land speculators, which helped spawn the "Squatter's Riot".

In 1851, he began editing his own newspaper, the *Settlers and Miners Tribune*. This newspaper survived but a few weeks. James worked for the *Sacramento Transcript*, *Democratic State Journal*, and the *Sacramento Times*, before joining John Rollin Ridge at the fledgling *Sacramento Bee*.

John Rollin Ridge wrote the fictional book, *The Life and Adventures of Joaquin Murietta, the Celebrated California Bandit*.

Less than a week after joining the Sacramento Bee, James McClatchy found himself in the position of editor.

That same week, the Bee reported a scandal that led to the impeachment of California State Treasurer, Henry Bates.

McClatchy made *The Bee* a bastion of progressive reformism. When James died in 1883 at age 59, his sons Charles Kenny McClatchy and V.S. McClatchy took over the paper.

The Bee is considered one of the oldest newspapers in the west and James McClatchy was one of its founding editors. The newspaper expanded its Central Valley coverage by founding the *Fresno Bee* in 1922, and the purchase of the *Modesto Bee* in 1927.

In 1979, the McClatchy newspaper empire expanded its coverage into the northwest with the purchase of the *Anchorage Daily News*. It purchased the *News Tribune* in Tacoma, Washington in 1986.

Eleanor McClatchy ran the newspaper chain from 1938 to 1978.

With a steady eye to growth, the McClatchy's bought three daily newspapers in South Carolina in 1990. It acquired *The News and Observer* in North Carolina in 1995.

In 1998, it added *The Star Tribune,* serving the Twin Cities of Minneapolis and St. Paul. The McClatchy group added the *Merced Sun-Star* in 2004.

In 2006, McClatchy became the second largest newspaper publisher in the United State by purchasing the Knight-Ridder chain of 32 daily papers.

Eleanor McClatchy, the youngest daughter of Charles Kenny McClatchy, was born in 1895. She was studying to become a playwright at Columbia University when her father asked her to take over the family business. At the time, it consisted of the

"Three Bees": the Sacramento Bee, the Fresno Bee and the Modesto Bee.

Under her administration, the Bee expanded to six daily newspapers and four radio stations. It also had one television station.

Eleanor McClatchy died in 1980.

Chapter 21

Dr. John F. Morse

Dr. John F. Morse

Dr. John F. Morse came to California from New York hoping to improve his own health. He tried gold mining for a brief time, but then opened a medical practice in Sacramento.

Dr. Morse and other doctors in Sacramento were soon faced with the cholera epidemic of 1850. He willingly helped those who could not pay. His generosity forced him to seek a second job to support his family. One of these jobs was selling real estate.

He ran for public office, owned a drugstore, and in 1851, was editor of the *Sacramento Union* newspaper. He wrote a vivid history of Sacramento. His writings gained him respect for his efforts to clean up Sacramento.

In writing about the buildings in which hospitals are housed, he wrote:

> *In the first place, we will find them located in buildings which, in situation, construction and finish, are entirely unsuited to the humane and glorious purpose for which they were produced.*
>
> *There is nothing to palliate or assuage the unmitigated popular meanness, nothing to redeem the despicable features of public economy, which is made the rule of action and the rod of inflexible law throughout the governmental and executive branches of county hospitals.*
>
> *The first result of this evil or crime is the adoption of the infamous system of selling off the poor and friendless sick at auction, not to the highest but to the lowest bidder.*
>
> *Now, of all the disgusting vices that make inroad upon the character of Christian communities, this to our*

mind is the most heathenish and unutterable cruelty that was ever inflicted upon the reputation of moral and accountable beings.

In an obituary about Dr. Morse, the Sacramento Union said,

Few men have had a larger or more laborious practice, but he continued a student to the time of his death, and he leaves no one in the State more thoroughly and familiarly acquainted with medical literature and science, their history, researches and latest results.

Dr. Morse opened a hospital at the corner of K and Third streets in Sacramento.

Chapter 22

Sacramento and Its Electric Power

Hydroelectric power

S acramento was one of the first cities in the United States to use hydroelectric power for commercial distribution. Hydroelectric power generation is an ideal source of electricity.

The process to produce power is based on water's physical strength. Water flows into tunnels, where it meets turbines and drives generators. The water then cleanly flows down river as usual.

It was gold mining that created the town of Folsom and indirectly led to the construction of the Folsom Powerhouse.

The man who first sought to harness the American River to generate power was Horatio Gates Livermore. He had control of the Natoma Water and Mining Company, a firm that had built a network of dams, ditches and reservoirs. This network supplied water to numerous gold mines in the American River area.

Old Folsom Powerhouse

Livermore wanted to go beyond that. He wanted to supply water power to operate a saw mill and other industries around Folsom.

In the mid-1860s, Livermore began construction on a dam to provide a holding pond for the logs cut in the higher foothills and sent down the river. He found the task more formidable than he anticipated.

Labor costs were expensive for quarrying the stone and building the dam and the system of canals and ditches. By the late 1880s, Livermore reached an agreement with state officials to provide Folsom prisoners to do the labor to build the dam.

Livermore died and his sons, Horatio P. and Charles E. pressed ahead with the dam construction and the sawmill project. Hydroelectric power generation was in its experimental stages.

The Livermores wanted to use it in their project. They built a canal 9,500 feet long across the American River. This would supply water power to four of the largest electric generators that had been built at the dam on the American River.

The bulkhead and head gates were finished in 1893.

Folsom state prison was the first to benefit from the dam when it put its own hydroelectric powerhouse into operation.

The Natomas main powerhouse complex was completed and ready to transmit power to Sacramento. It consisted of four 750 kilowatt electrical generators, or dynamos, each more than eight feet high. These generators weighed 57,000 pounds.

Driving these generators were four McCormick dual turbines with a capacity of 1260 horsepower for each pair. These turbines were driven by water surging through four eight-foot diameter penstocks.

Sacramento celebrated the event by stringing electric lights along each of its downtown streets and decorating the State Capitol Building with thousands of bulbs. The event caught not only the attention of the state but of the nation as well.

Chapter 23

The Ship Race

The New World side-wheeler commanded the river.

The steamboat *Washoe* was designed to challenge the monopoly of the California Steam Navigation Company. Unfortunately, the Washoe's design was faulty and it lost more than 130 passengers in one of the most tragic accidents on the Sacramento River.

The story of the *Washoe* began a year before at the Hunter's Point shipyard in San Francisco.

Since 1854, the California Steam Navigation Company determined not only the rates but the schedules for all steamboats on the Sacramento and San Joaquin rivers.

The Side-wheeler Antelope was a river favorite.

The rivers were a favored route to and from the gold fields and the towns growing along the Sacramento and San Joaquin rivers.

One of the most famous river steamers was the *Antelope*. This side-wheeler was one hundred and fifty feet long and carried 300 passengers.

Aided by her sleek design and excellent captains, the *Antelope* gained a reputation as the fastest and most reliable steamboat on the early San Francisco to Sacramento run.

The *Antelope* had a schedule that she proudly kept. She departed San Francisco on Mondays, Wednesdays and Fridays promptly at 4 p.m. She left Sacramento at 2 p.m. on the following day to make her return run.

In 1854, Wells Fargo had a huge and growing problem. The express company needed to transport a huge amount of gold coming out of the Sierra Nevada mines to San Francisco.

Gold Dust and bullion were pouring out of the hills. But the gold fields were also filled with cutthroats and robbers such as Tom Bell and Rattlesnake Dick who wanted to get their hands on the gold.

Stagecoaches and lone travelers were routinely robbed. Wells Fargo decided it needed a fast, dependable steamship on which to transport the gold from Sacramento to San Francisco.

The *Antelope* was captained by her owner, David Van Pelt, and she became the obvious choice of Wells Fargo to haul its gold. Travelers, such as entertainer Lola Montez also preferred the *Antelope*.

She was known up and down the river as a "lucky" boat. Unlike other steamers, the *Antelope* had never suffered a boiler explosion or other mishap.

Her only accident during her lifetime was when she rammed a steamer by the name of *Confidence* in Suisun Bay during a dense fog. No lives were lost and the passengers sustained only miner bruises.

A unique Wells Fargo messenger's compartment was constructed on the Antelope. That room became known as the "Gold Room". The floor of this treasure room was heavily reinforced and braced to withstand the weight of the heavy shipments of gold.

Each shipment was accompanied by heavily armed guards. The *Antelope* stopped in Martinez for passengers and then steamed on through the Carquinez Straits to San Francisco.

The *Antelope* never lost a single flake of gold to theft, robbers or accident.

In 1861, a new challenger appeared on the river. A steamship captain named Kidd appeared with his steamship *Nevada*. The California Navigation Company was unimpressed, but neither did it welcome the competition.

The company began an effort to force Kidd off the river. The first challenge came from the company's steamer *New World*. It forced the *Nevada* onto a mud bank.

A rematch between the *New World* and the *Nevada* came in 1863. The two boats raced neck-and-neck as they steamed into Steamboat Slough above Rio Vista.

The pilot of the *Nevada* failed to notice an ominous swirl in the water ahead. A submerged snag caught the *Nevada*. The *Nevada* began to fill with water.

The passengers were able to swim to shore, but the Nevada was not so fortunate. It was a total loss.

Captain Kidd was determined to continue the rivalry with the Navigation Company.

Kidd decided he would design a steamboat adapted to the river and capable of challenging the monopoly held by the Navigation Company.

This new boat would be called the *Washoe*. There was general consensus that design and workmanship were near perfect. Captain Kidd hired engineer Edward Foster to supervise the construction.

The Sacramento company of Goss and Lombard built the machinery to fit Kidd's specifications. The contract called for two engines, each having twenty-two cylinders, a stroke of seven feet, and 150 horsepower.

The boat's most distinguishing feature was the four boilers. Each was 32-feet long and 40-inches in diameter, capable of holding 150 pounds of pressure.

According to Henry Floyd, who built the boilers, they were made of the best iron "I ever used in a boiler".

The *Washoe* began her initial run to Sacramento at 11 a.m., May 7, 1864. She carried 250 passengers and crew, as well as some official observers responsible for the construction of the steamboat.

The observers noted that as the *Washoe* left her birth, the flues were leaking at the rivets and a little around the flanges, as well as in some seams of the boilers.

Goss claimed that all boilers leak at first, but not quite as much as those aboard the Washoe.

The journey to Sacramento was completed without incident. It was a happy occasion when the Washoe arrived at the foot of L Street. It appeared that finally, here was a steamer that could challenge the Navigation Company.

After its return to San Francisco, the *Washoe* began regular runs between San Francisco and Sacramento. Each Monday, Wednesday and Friday, at 4 p.m. it started upriver on the same schedule as the *Antelope*.

The *Washoe* arrived in Sacramento six hours later. On the return trip, it left Sacramento at noon on Tuesday, Thursday and Saturday. Sunday was used for routine maintenance and upkeep.

It soon became apparent to the Navigation Company that the *Washoe* was a serious competitor for the riverboat trade.

The California Navigation scheduled the queen of its fleet, the *Chrysopolis*, to make the same run as the *Washoe*. In addition, it scheduled the *Yosemite* to run on alternate days. The company was now scheduling service between Sacramento and San Francisco six days a week.

The first impact between the California Navigation Company and Captain Kidd's company was reduced fares. Kidd had been charging passengers three dollars for a cabin and two dollars for deck accommodations.

The Navigation Company undercut him by drastically reducing its rates to 50 cents for a cabin and 25 cents for deck.

Captain Kidd could not meet these new rates and still maintain his boat. He continued to operate for a few days and then decided to take his boat from the water for some needed repairs.

Rumors spread that the monopoly had bought off Captain Kidd when he stopped making his scheduled runs. Kidd fought back. He took out an ad in the *Alta California* newspaper stating why his boat was not making its normal runs.

Repairs will necessitate a delay of
6 to 12 days, which will probably give
the public an opportunity of traveling

at old rates again, a luxury of which
we have been deprived for two weeks.

As Kidd predicted, the Navigation Company raised its rates to three dollars for a cabin and two dollars for deck accommodations.

The delay that Kidd had foreseen stretched into five weeks. The boilers and flues on the Washoe were completely overhauled. Inspector Beemis tested the boilers at 210 pounds with no sign of leaking.

He issued a certificate allowing the Washoe to run under a maximum pressure of 140 pounds.

The fierce competition from the monopoly and the brash intruder erupted again. The monopoly lowered its rates to two dollars and one dollar. Kidd matched those rates.

It appeared evident that a physical encounter might ensue in the battle of the river. On July 1, the *Washoe* approached Benicia landing from San Francisco, while the Navigation Company's *Yosemite* was about the same distance away on the Sacramento side.

When the captains of each boat noted their situations, they raced for Benicia. The inevitable collision occurred at the landing. The *Washoe* began taking on water and backed into shallower waters to avoid sinking.

Reports from the boats differed. Those from the *Washoe* claimed it had reached the landing first and had made fast before the *Yosemite* stopped its engines only 50 feet from the land and at no time reversed its paddles.

After the collision, the *Yosemite* made fast to the landing, took on passengers and departed, making no effort to offer assistance to the damaged *Washoe*.

Kidd repaired the damage to his boat and entered the fray again. Fate seemed to go against Captain Kidd. Boiler troubles began again as leaks developed around the patches installed earlier.

Kidd had his vessel hauled off the river to make new repairs. When he resumed his regular run he found leaking flues prevented engineers and firemen from maintaining more than 50 pounds of pressure.

When the boilers began leaking water faster than pumps could supply it, the crew was forced to extinguish the fires a short distance below Rio Vista.

The Washoe made repairs, but reached Sacramento twelve hours late. Captain Kidd got his boat back to San Francisco and employed a different foundry to make the repairs.

He put the *Washoe* back in service on August 25. He decided to compete directly with the *Yosemite* rather than the *Chrysopolis*. Throughout the afternoon of August 30, excitement at the San Francisco wharves was at a high pitch.

The *Yosemite* transferred all of her freight to the Antelope and was stripped for speed. The *Washoe* carried just enough freight to give her a proper trim.

Within minutes of each other, four steamers, the *Washoe* and three Navigation Company steamers, the *Yosemite*, the *Antelope* and *Paul Pry*, departed from the San Francisco wharves.

The *Yosemite* and *Antelope* led through the choppy waters with their deeper draught. It was evident though, that the *Washoe* fully intended to make a race of it.

The Washoe overtook the two steamers when it reached the smoother water of San Pablo Bay and reached Benicia 14 minutes ahead of the Navigation Company's vessels.

After touching at Rio Vista to take on passengers, the *Washoe* was reentering the channel as the *Yosemite* approached. The Yosemite started blowing its whistle signaling for the *Washoe* to stop.

Captain Kidd, rather than stopping, maneuvered his boat close to the left bank to allow the *Yosemite* room to pass.

The two boats raced alongside each other for about a half mile and then the *Yosemite* turned into the *Washoe*, striking her just forward of the wheelhouse.

The Washoe's paddlewheels were undamaged, but much of her upper works were demolished, including two staterooms and a store room. The *Washoe* continued upriver, now running far behind the *Yosemite*.

The following day, each boat made its run without incident. Captain Kidd again had to take his vessel off the river for repairs. It returned to the river September 5, 1864, to make its most fateful trip.

As departure time neared, the *Chrysopolis* and *Antelope* had left their berths. Captain Kidd briefed his engineers, asking them to carry a light head of steam because there was no hurry.

As the *Washoe* backed out of its berth, most of the 153 passengers were watching the crew, waving to their friends and conversing among themselves.

131

As the *Washoe* left the bay and entered the river, she drew alongside the *Antelope*. The engineers allowed the steam pressure to rise in the boilers to 135 pounds to test for leaks. The pressure was then reduced to 100 pounds.

Captain Kidd made stops at Benicia, Collinsville and Rio Vista to take on passengers. At Benicia, he was informed that the Chrysopolis was about 45 minutes ahead.

After leaving Rio Vista, without warning, the *Washoe* exploded. Engineer Phillips was slammed to the deck. Hissing steam, splintering wood and cries of agony resounded on the *Washoe*.

The loss of the steering gear in the explosion and the boat's forward momentum caused the *Washoe* to run aground.

One man, who escaped through a broken window, and another passenger, cut a small boat loose and lowered it to the water. They picked up several survivors.

After three hours, help arrived in the form of the *Antelope* who rounded the bend and saw the calamitous wreckage. Captain Albert Foster nosed his boat into the bank and took the injured and dying aboard.

The *Antelope* departed three hours later, her decks littered with the grisly aftermath of the *Washoe* explosion.

When the Antelope arrived in Sacramento, the owners of the Vernon house made the building available as a hospital.

The Navigation Company dispatched its steamboat, the *Visalia*, to the wreck of the *Washoe* to render assistance. The wrecked hull of the

Washoe was resting on the bottom at an odd angle. The stern, pointing upstream, was submerged nearly to the hurricane deck.

When the Visalia crew boarded the wrecked *Washoe*, they found Captain Kidd and some crew members searching for bodies.

The haggard Captain Kidd clearly showed the effects of the wreck. He suggested the *Visalia* take the recovered bodies back to Sacramento.

Captain Kidd sent a $1,000 check to Howard Benevolent Society, who cared for the victims of the wreck.

He then began trying to raise the sunken *Washoe*. He employed three ships and their crews to raise the steamer. Three days later, the *Washoe* was afloat.

Divers were sent down to plug the hole in the starboard wheelhouse so that pumps could rid the hull of water. Inspection showed the *Washoe* was sound except for the massive hole in the wheelhouse.

When word reached Sacramento that the *Washoe* was afloat, the coroner's jury made another inspection of the Washoe's boilers.

Captain Kidd was facing some new troubles. Passengers brought suit against the steamer *Washoe* and Captain Kidd in the Sacramento County Court.

The suit asked $10,000 each in damages and costs of the lawsuit. Court records don't reflect a judgment in the suit, so it was likely settled out of court.

On the same day the *Washoe* was being towed to San Francisco, Kidd said all four boilers would be replaced with new ones of a different design.

By February 1865, the *Washoe* was back in service. It was no longer the glamorous river steamer, but a pedestrian ferryboat.

In 1878, it was taken out of service and broken up.

Chapter 24
Weinstock

Weinstock's occupied an imposing building on K Street, which, while only three stories in height, featured an imposing arched entryway.

Harris Weinstock was one of the busiest men in Old Sacramento. David Lubin, a Polish émigré via New York, built the Mechanic's Store in 1874 in Sacramento. The store's space measured 16 by 24 feet.

When Lubin opened the Mechanic's Store, he was charting new territory. He settled into the small store space. He made shelves and set up a counter from the dry goods boxes covered with an oil cloth.

He hung out his sign:

D. Lubin, ONE PRICE—Weinstock's: Sacramento's Finest Department Store.

David Lubin and Harris Weinstock

Lubin was an inventor and held several patents. One such patent was for the *endless fly overall.*

Railroad workers complained to Rubin about the inferiority of the overalls he was receiving from his supplier. The overalls had a tendency to split open at the crotch.

When Rubin saw a problem, he was inclined to walk straight into it and do something about it.

Lubin designed a pair of overalls with an innovation that prevented them from splitting open. He hired workers, supplied them with sewing machines, and manufactured the overalls in Sacramento.

He sold them to railroad workers for half the price of the riveted overalls they had been getting.

In 1888, The Mechanic's Store incorporated as the Weinstock-Lubin Company. It went on to become the West's largest department store.

Harris Weinstock served as Market Director for the state of California. (It was later changed to California Director of Agriculture).

He was an instigator in the formation of grower associations. Weinstock was a member of the American Commission charged with investigating farm finance and cooperative credit in Europe.

The Weinstock-Lubin department store was on the southeast corner of Fourth and K streets. It measured 120 feet by 160 feet. It featured theatrical window displays, a unique children's department, and a touch of big city fashion.

Weinstock-Lubin transacted much of their business by mail, necessitating the hiring of 250 to 320 employees. Weinstock-Lubin had offices in New York City, San Francisco and other large cities.

Weinstock Lubin & Co. was an early adopter of the eight-hour work day. The partners set up a profit sharing program with their employees. They divided their employees into four grades.

The first grade employees were permitted to be stockholders. The second grade workers were heads of the various departments. The third grade employees held subordinate positions, having served a certain length of time. The fourth grade included the remainder of the store's employees.

Promotion of employees was strictly on merit. A ledger with an account of each employee was kept. The employers imposed small fines on employees for shortcomings.

The profit-sharing fund was divided *pro rata* among the class from which it had risen.

Weinstock and Rubin encouraged their employees to further their education. An

137

educational department was created and teachers employed for the different branches.

All persons under the age of 17 were able to benefit from this company-sponsored education to further their skills in writing and math.

In 1903, the downtown Sacramento store was destroyed by fire. A fireman was killed. The company didn't hesitate. It built a new store which was the biggest in Sacramento.

David Lubin became impatient. He wanted to do more than just run a family department store and mail-order house. He let Harris Weinstock become CEO of Weinstock-Lubin and Company.

Lubin, meanwhile, engaged in agriculture. He started orchards in the Sacramento area, and brought European farming methods to the area. He helped found the California Fruit Growers Union.

He then helped settle Eastern European Jewish refugees who worked on various farms. In 1891, Lubin became the director of the International Society for the Colonization of Russian Jews.

Lubin campaigned for subsidies and protection of farms, initially in California and then on an international scale. His son, Simon, helped him develop a proposal for an international chamber of agriculture.

In 1896, he moved to Europe to implement his proposal. In May 1908, with the sponsorship of Italy's King Victor Emmanuel III, the International Institute of Agriculture opened in Rome.

In 1949, Weinstock Lubin & Company was acquired by its arch rival, Hale Bros. In 1979, the new parent company Carter Hawley Hales Stores expanded Weinstock & Company into Reno, Nevada and Salt Lake City, Utah.

What happened to Weinstock Lubin & Company?

Once a powerful retailer in Central California, it became a part of Hale Bros., which later merged with Broadway Stores and became Broadway Hale. Broadway Hale merged with Emporium Capwell to become Carter Hawley Hales Stores.

Wall Street jokingly called the new company EGO, Inc.

As it went on to acquire new stores in an effort to become the biggest retail chain in the U.S., it became heavily in debt. Macy's became a better competitor in California and Nordstrom's entered the market.

A host of specialty retailers and big box stores made the store divisions of Carter Hawley Hale no longer relevant to customers. Carter Hawley Hale Stores were sold to an investor group, Zell/Chilmark.

Mistakes made by this investor group finished off the parent company and resulted in the 1995 sale to Federated Department Stores. With this sale, all divisions, including Weinstocks were either converted to Macy's or sold.

Chapter 25

Sacramento's
Japanese Community

Sacramento's Japanese Community

The first Japanese in Sacramento may have been those headed for the Gold Hill Silk Colony near Coloma. When that colony collapsed for lack of water, some of the Japanese who settled there may have returned to reside in Sacramento.

It is certain that twelve Japanese people did live in Sacramento in 1883. Their numbers increased slowly because the Japanese government restricted large-scale emigration until 1884.

Issei settled in Walnut Grove which is in the San Joaquin Delta south of Sacramento.

By 1891, about one thousand Japanese arrived in the United States, with one hundred of them settling in Sacramento. By 1910, there were close to 4,000 throughout California.

The Sacramento Bee reported that seven hundred Japanese gathered in McKinley Park to celebrate a victory of their motherland over China. It is believed that many of these celebrants were migrant farm workers working in the Sacramento Valley.

By 1911, Sacramento had more than two-hundred Japanese-owned businesses. These included hotels, boarding houses, restaurants, barber shops, pool and billiard parlors, retail shops, a newspaper and a movie theater.

142

Japanese-American farm workers work at the Tule Lake Relocation center in Newell, California, during World War II.

These businesses all conducted their financial business with a Japanese-owned bank. In addition, Japanese worked in Sacramento as cooks, domestic servants and as porters.

When there were only a few Japanese in the area, working as farm laborers, the white populace tolerated them well-enough. In 1893, the *Sacramento Bee* approvingly called the Japanese "more docile and obedient" than the Chinese.

As they expanded into different areas of employment, anti-Japanese sentiment among the white citizenry grew. By 1907, significant labor controversies broke out involving Japanese barbers and laundrymen.

In one incident in Oak Park, a mob attacked a Japanese laundry.

In 1908, the Asiatic Exclusion League of North America formed a chapter in Sacramento. In 1909, five anti-Japanese measures were introduced in the legislature although none of them passed.

In the agricultural fields there were conflicting sentiments. The white landowners wanted the Japanese as farm laborers, or at most, tenant farmers. They did not want them as competing landowners.

The thrifty and industrious Japanese soon acquired their own small truck farms and operated them profitably. This led to anti-Japanese sentiment and the passage of the Alien Land Law in 1913.

The Alien Land Law prevented "aliens ineligible to citizenship—the Japanese—from own land in California. It did not prevent them from leasing land for periods of up to three years.

It also did not prevent them from registering land in the name of their American-born children. The law mollified anti-Japanese forces for a while. But by 1920, it was realized that loopholes still allowed the Japanese to compete with whites in agriculture.

That year, a statewide initiative effectively blocking Japanese ownership of farmland passed in California by a three-to-one margin.

There were some who feared the Japanese were attempting to overtake white control of California farmland. The enactment of this law had the effect of decreasing Japanese control of farmland by 40 per cent.

There were at least sixteen prosecutions of Japanese for violations of the Alien Land Law from 1920 to 1940.

The Alien Land Laws were invalidated in 1952 by the Supreme Court of California as a violation of the equal protection clause of the 14th amendment to the United States Constitution.

The typical Issei (first generation Japanese immigrants to America) was a single man who came to California to make money. He hoped to take enough cash home for both he and his family to live a comfortable life.

Japanese coming to America did not find an easy life awaiting them. Only about one Issei in six received any form of assistance from organizations such as churches to help them get started.

Issei considered it shameful to be a burden to someone else or receive grants from the government.

Chapter 26

Wells Fargo

Lloyd Tevis, of Wells Fargo

L loyd Tevis learned early in life the importance of investing. He came to California in 1849 during the gold rush. He failed when it came to digging for gold but he found huge success as a banker.

After his stint at panning for gold, he went to Sacramento and was hired by the county recorder's office. Before coming to California, Tevis studied law and worked as a court clerk for his father.

James Ben Ali Haggin

Tevis saved his money and soon purchased a Sacramento lot for $250. He next opened a law office with a new acquaintance, James Ben Ali Haggin. They moved their law office to San Francisco in 1853.

Haggin and Tevis acquired Rancho Del Paso, a land grant near Sacramento. The two partners then married sisters, the daughters of Colonel Lewis Sanders, a Kentuckian who immigrated to California.

Tevis was one of the principal owners of the California Steam Navigation Company and one of the projectors of telegraphy lines throughout California.

In his negotiations to sell California State Telegraph Company to Western Union Telegraph Company, his profits and commissions amounted to $200,000.

Henry Wells founded American Express Company and Wells Fargo Bank.

At one time Tevis owned thirteen hundred miles of stagecoach lines in California. He also had horse-drawn streetcars in San Francisco, and ranch lands with thousands of cattle and sheep.

Tevis was a pioneer in the reclamation of tule and swamp lands in central California.

Wells Fargo and Company was officially organized March 18, 1852. Its stated purpose was to provide express and banking services to California.

Tevis was elected president of Wells Fargo in 1872, a capacity he held for 20 years. Tevis boasted one time that he could think five times as fast as any man in San Francisco. He often proved it. In his later years, he apparently relaxed his banking practices too much.

An extensive audit in 1891 was critical of Tevis's banking affairs. He was forced out as president of Wells Fargo. Further pressure resulted in his resigning completely from the banking operation.

Wells Fargo began by using stage lines already in operation. It soon developed its familiar red Wells Fargo stagecoaches.

Wells Fargo history goes back farther. Wells and Company was a New York firm. In 1844, Wells hired William G. Fargo as a paid messenger to make use of lake steamers in the summer and wagons in the winter.

In 1850, the route between Albany and Buffalo, New York led to the merger of Wells & Company; Butterfield, Wasson & Company; and Livingston, Fargo & Company. The merger formed the American Express Company.

Wells became president and Fargo was treasurer. When the gold rush news in California arrived in the east, all eyes turned westward.

Wells Fargo sent two agents to California. Agent Samuel P. Carter arrived June 27, 1852. He was charged with opening a General Express Forwarding Agency.

A bulletin in the *Daily Alta California* announced Wells Fargo would purchase and sell "Gold Dust, Bullion and Bills of Exchange". In addition, it would handle the collection of gold dust, bullion and specie, in addition to forwarding packages, parcels and freight between San Francisco and New York.

Wells Fargo said it would also handle shipments to cities and towns throughout California. The company assured customers that armed agents would travel with all shipments and offer the same protection traveling east.

The company did not become involved in handling money until its representative Rueben W. Washburn arrived in San Francisco aboard the steamer Tennessee. Washburn's first exchange was on July 13, 1852, marking the beginning of Wells Fargo's banking business.

Henry Wells made his first trip to California in 1853. He wrote a letter to Wells Fargo president Colonel Edwin Morgan on the progress and success of Samuel Carter and Reuben Washburn.

> *Our Internal Express here is one of the most profitable that I ever knew for its age. I am perfectly satisfied with all Carter's arrangements. They have been judicious and well-timed, liberal but not extravagant & as such have given me the confidence of the best men of the Town.*
>
> *You may recollect Brigham of the Harnden Express was spoken of & he has kindly offered to take charge of our interests here in connection with the Vanderbilt line of steamers at the moderate salary of Ten Thousand a Year. Carter is worth two of him. In fact he is the man for the position...but he will want to come back & remain in the east.*
>
> *This is a great Country & a greater people. Our Express is just in from Sacramento & the mines & our*

Waybill for New York will amount to nearly $3,000. The amount going forward by this steamer as you will see is the largest ever shipped from this Port. Had the express got in from the Southern mines we should have had some Two-hundred Ounces more to add to our amount.

Within six years after the discovery of gold, California was no longer the land of plenty. Disgruntled miners were returning from the gold fields empty-handed.

By February of 1855, unsound speculation in the financial world cause the California banking system to collapse and Wells Fargo faced its first crisis.

A run on Page, Bacon & Company, a San Francisco bank, began when its parent bank in St. Louis collapsed. The run spread to other financial institutions, all of which, including Wells Fargo, closed their doors.

Wells Fargo reopened its doors within a week. It was one of the few banking/express companies to survive the panic because it kept sufficient assets on hand to meet the demand.

As a survivor of the panic, Wells Fargo had the advantage of eliminating competition and achieving a reputation for dependability.

In the 1860s, Wells Fargo had 147 offices in California. It had a monopoly on the express business, and with its fancy Concord coaches, became the proprietor of the greatest stagecoach empire in the country.

The stage line had its rules:

1. *When the driver asks you to get off and walk, do so without grumbling. He won't request it unless absolutely necessary.*
2. *If the team runs away, sit still and take your chances. If you jump, nine times out of ten you will get hurt.*
3. *Don't smoke a strong pipe inside the coach— spit on the leeward side.*
4. *If you have anything to drink in a bottle, pass it around.*
5. *Never shoot on the road as the noise may frighten the horses.*
6. *Don't discuss politics or religion.*
7. *Don't point out where murders have been committed if there are women passengers.*
8. *Don't imagine for a moment that you are going on a picnic. Expect annoyances, discomfort, and some hardship.*

Completion of the Continental Railroad in 1869 brought about the demise of the stage business and a decline in Wells Fargo stock.

Lloyd Tevis organized the Pacific Union Express Company to compete with Wells Fargo. William Fargo, his brother Charles Fargo, and Ashbel Barney negotiated a deal with Tevis to buy Pacific Union Express.

Chapter 27

The California State Fair

(San Francisco Chronicle, December 11, 1873)

This poster appeared in San Francisco Chronicle December 11, 1873

The *Alta California* urged the formation of an agricultural society to enhance California's reputation as an ideal place for farming and industry.

California's legislature was quick to meet the challenge. It created the State Agricultural Society in 1852. Eighty enthusiastic people signed up for the initial effort to plan an agricultural exposition.

This pig welcomes his entry in state fair.

The California State Fair was held in San Francisco in 1854. Travel and hardship caused organizers to move the fair's locations each year. It was next held in Sacramento, then San Jose, next in Stockton and then in Marysville.

Marysville hosted the fair for four years in a row. The fair became the yearly source of entertainment and education for early settlers, drawing as many as 15,000 visitors on a single day.

When the California State Fair returned to Sacramento in 1859, it was decided by organizers to find a permanent home for it. Sacramento was a bustling city with 2,500 buildings and a newly installed water system.

The water system used two-and-a-half miles of pipe.

Organizers were able to buy sixe square blocks of property between E and H streets. The money to purchase the land came through a special election and contributions from local citizens.

The site for the fair was called *Capitol Park*. Capitol Park is now the site of the California State Capitol Building.

Horses played a significant role in the state fair. It was the horse that helped develop the west. The horse also provided transportation and entertainment.

California's role in the breeding of fine horses and the development of the sport of horse racing led the way.

By the turn of the century, the popularity and growth of the State Fair forced organizers to find a larger site. The Capitol Park location was sold and the State Agricultural Society purchased 100 acres southeast of the city limits on Stockton Boulevard, which opened in the summer of 1909.

For the next 58 years, the California State Fair evolved and flourished. Agriculture increased and several hundred men were working in the harvest fields.

"I had to kill four or sometimes five oxen daily to feed them. I could raise 40,000 bushels of wheat without trouble, reap the crops with sickles, thresh it with bones and winnow it in the wind," said Kent Ruth, in his book, *Great Day in the West*.

The fair features in 1854 were two-inch long peanuts, 72-pound sugar beets, and a 10-pound carrot measuring three feet long. The fair then introduced thrill shows and contests to liven up the event.

157

It was in the 1870s that California's counties began creating exhibits to showcase their "bragging rights" against each other. This competition continues today and are among the most popular exhibits at the fair.

At the turn of the century, organizers staged a train wreck, delighting spectators as two locomotives crashed, creating masses of twisted, steaming steel.

This demonstration was a huge hit and continued until the beginning of World War I.

Carnival rides were introduced just prior to World War I.

In the early years, exhibitors brought their livestock to the fair by rail. Today, the fair hosts competitions in biotechnology such as DNA analysis.

For its centennial in 1954, ten thousand ladies were give free orchids. Dancing waters became a new attraction.

Entertainment featured such acts as Jack Benny, Peggy Lee, Bob Hope, Abbott and Costello and Duke Ellington's orchestra.

One of three operational monorails in the country is at the California State Fair. It operates a demonstration farm and a Forest Center.

A nice feature is the fair's lagoon, situated in the middle of the property.

The California Exposition and State Fair (Cal Expo) is an independent state agency established by law in California food and agriculture codes. It's governed by an 11-member board of directors.

During the fair, more than 2,000 seasonal temporary workers are hired. The fair receives no money from government funding and operates as a self-sufficient entity.

The California State Fair now sits on 356 acres adjacent to the American River.

Chapter 28

New Innovations
For Sacramento

An 1879 telephone.

After Alexander Graham Bell invented the telephone in 1876, it soon showed up in Sacramento. At first, the new gadgets were curiosities.

By 1879, the city had a five-mile continuous telephone line that connected twenty-nine businesses to a central switchboard.

In the same year, Sacramentans would see electric lighting. In a special display during California State Fair week, electricity generated by the steam presses of the *Sacramento Union* lit up display windows at the neighboring Weinstock-Lubin Department Store.

A number of Sacramento industries used steam-generated electricity to run machinery, especially in the railroad workshops, the H. Fisher candy factory, and clothing manufacturers.

The high cost of coal, which was imported from British Columbia, limited its availability.

In 1895, the transmission of electricity from Folsom to Sacramento happened. Electrical engineers at the time believed that five miles was the furthest distance electric power could be sent.

Horatio Gates Livermore believed differently. Livermore had already dammed the American River near Folsom to form a mill pond for logging.

He believed the dam could provide hydroelectric power as well as serving the logging industry.

Before beginning work on a hydroelectric facility in 1892, Livermore obtained a franchise to build an electric street car system in Sacramento. He incorporated the Sacramento Electric Power and Light Company.

Howard Gallatin, general manager of the Huntington and Hopkins Hardware Store provided much of the financial backing.

Livermore built the Folsom Powerhouse and two parallel transmission lines over twenty-two miles to downtown Sacramento. There were a few false starts, but he transmitted eleven thousand volts of electricity on the morning of July 13, 1895.

This was the longest transmission of electricity in the world at that time.

In the 1880s, Sacramentans saw a new means of transportation exhibited. This was arrival of the bicycle. Suddenly, individuals could propel themselves around town more swiftly than on foot or in horse-drawn carriages.

The Capitol City Wheelmen in 1903.

With its sixty-inch front wheel and a six-inch rear wheel, the general public wasn't too interested. It was hazardous to mount one these bicycles and difficult to propel as the rider had to move the front wheel directly with his feet.

The Capitol City Wheelmen coordinated with other groups and lobbied for improvements that led to a paved road from Sacramento to Folsom suitable for bicycle excursions.

By the end of the century, the Wheelmen were able to push the "Good Roads" movement and influence the shape of the state's early highway plans.

On March 30, 1896, members of the Capital City Wheelmen voted to build a bicycle path from Sacramento to Folsom. Each member was assessed one dollar. Sacramento merchants and citizens donated $900 to begin the path's construction.

Five hundred bicyclists rode the first section of the path on April 12, 1896.

Chapter 29

Old Sacramento's Underground Tunnels

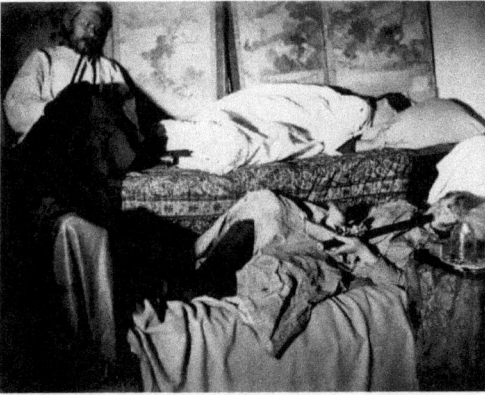

An opium den in San Francisco's underground. A similar underground existed in Old Sacramento

A labyrinth of tunnels permeates Old Sacramento's underground. Floods from the Sacramento River damaged the goods and properties of the business in town. They decided to fix the problem in 1862 by raising the level of the streets.

On January 10, newly elected governor Leland Stanford had to travel to the Capitol by boat for his inauguration. The flooding was considered so dangerous the legislature abandoned Sacramento for San Francisco. Residents fled for safety.

Storefront in Old Sacramento today.

Brick walls that form part of the underground tunnels in old Sacramento.

Hidden beneath the City of Old Sacramento for nearly 150 years, its underground is its best kept secret.

Plans were made to raise the streets to continue Sacramento's urban growth.

Sacramento was the first city on the West Coast. It's the only city in California to raise its street level. This was a tremendous feat for the thirteen-year-old city.

Mark Twain chimed in with his criticism of the street-raising project. "The system of raising its buildings has its advantages. It makes the floor shady and this is something that is great in such a warm climate. It also enables the inquiring stranger to rest his elbows on the second-story windows and look in and criticize the bedroom arrangements of all the citizens."

The original waterfront of the town, part of which has been preserved as the Old Town Sacramento District, does not sit at ground level.

The storm inadvertently created Old Sacramento's underground.

The lower level did not vanish. It simply became invisible to those who lacked access to the tunnels. The streets were raised about 10 feet and the new underground spaces were created. Merchants used some of the space as storage.

A Chinese herbalist used the space to conduct business.

The tunnels were not always used for legitimate activities. They served as homes for prostitution and as opium dens. Much like the tunnels in Portland, Oregon, these tunnels eventually gained a reputation for being the dwellings of unnatural horrors.

One rumor holds that even transients will not sleep in the tunnels due to constant feelings of being threatened by some unseen force.

There is little specific information in the literature to describe how the tunnels were used after the streets were raised.

Chapter 30

The Prison Ship

The La Grange, Sacramento's Prison Ship

It was a ship used to house prisoner's in Sacramento, but it sometimes did double duty. One such case was when Samuel Garrett and Harriett Brickel, used it as a chapel for their wedding ceremony.

Sam, the groom, was being held in close confinement in the prison brig *La Grange*.

A large crowd watched as Justice C.C. Jenks stood solemnly on the foredeck and joined the youthful couple in a brief but holy matrimony.

One thing is sure. Harriet's father did not give the bride away. He was dead, shot down in the street in front of the Golden Eagle Hotel. The bridegroom Sam did the shooting.

People knew that Amiel Brickel, Harriet's father, was difficult to get along with. Even Amiel's wife confided that if she could just see Harriett safely married, she wouldn't spend another minute under the same roof with her cantankerous husband.

Amiel Brickel didn't take kindly to Sam Garrett's attentions to his daughter.

A teamster friend of Amiel's testified that Harriett had been beaten "enough by her father to kill and ox".

Matters came to a head when Sam and Harriett moved into the Golden Eagle Hotel, posing as man and wife. Brickel then met Garrett in front of the hotel. Brickel called Sam "a damned thieving *son-of-a-bitch*".

These harsh words still didn't provoke Sam into action. The next day, when the couple came downstairs for breakfast, Garrett left Harriett in the dining room.

Garrett, with gun in hand, stepped outside to face the girl's father. Brickel rose and began walking toward the motionless Garrett. Sam warned Brickel to "Keep away! Don't come near me, God damn you! I have run from you as long as I intend to."

Brickel made no reply, but continued his advance on Garrett. Witnesses testified that Brickel held his hand inside his coat as he came toward Garrett. Sam began firing. Five heavy slugs from Garrett's Navy revolver tore through Brickel.

Brickel dropped lifeless on the plank sidewalk. He wasn't carrying a gun.

Garrett was tried, convicted, and sentenced to hang. An appeal was taken to the State Supreme Court. It upheld Garrett's conviction and a new date for execution was set.

Harriett Brickel, in despair over her husband's impending execution, tried to end her own life by taking poison.

Five days after his wedding, Garrett was removed from his cell. He was taken by wagon to his place of execution near Sutter's Fort. He was hanged by the neck. He was not yet 23 years old.

In 1850, Sacramento's Court of Quarterly Sessions was given the authority to build a county jail. Prison brigs were Sacramento's novel solution to the jail problem.

The *La Grange* was the third and last of Sacramento's floating jails. The city authorized $2,500 for the purchase of the La Grange. The ship was ordered to be moored at the mouth of the American River, upstream from H Street.

Once in place, another $2,500 was authorized for repairs and alterations. The hold was partitioned into cells and a superstructure was added topside to properly fit the vessel out as a jail.

On the La Grange, the forward cabin, strongly built of solid oak, was used as a dungeon. Iron shafts were embedded into the oaken planks that extended the full height of the cells to which the prisoners were shackled every night.

This, in addition to a ball and chain riveted to the leg of each prisoner, was calculated to discourage escapes.

La Grange proved to be far from escape-proof. An 1851 newspaper article said:

> *Up to a late period, it was tantamount to an escape for any malefactor to be sent on this vessel, so easy was the way of getting out.*

Not all of the miscreants made their escape good. Captain-in-Charge James McDonald recalled one escape attempt made in 1852:

> *Now and then a man escaped, but swimming ashore with shackles on was a risky business and only the most desperate characters ever attempted it.*
>
> *But, in the summer of 1852, three convicts removed a bar from a port and escaped without a sound. The bar was held in place with huge iron staples, but the three fashioned a windlass and pulled the staples loose.*
>
> *Although wearing leg irons, they started to swim to shore. Two escaped but were recaptured later. The third didn't make it. He drowned.*
>
> *Escapes were attempted many times and at least one a year was successful. Some years there were as many as four to five successful escapes.*

Sacramento's County Board of Supervisors wanted to ensure that escapes from the *La Grange* were not made easier by corrupt or lax practices. It was decreed by the Court of Sessions that $500 would be deducted from money allocated to the sheriff for each escape.

The State followed suit with a new law which charged a sheriff or jailor permitting an escape with a misdemeanor and a fine of up to $20,000.

Sacramento's Board of Supervisors adopted a policy of putting prisoners to work to defray the cost of running the jail. Concerns grew about using the decomposing hulk *La Grange* as a prison.

An 1855 editorial stated:

> *It is questionable whether the old hulk La Grange which has so long been used for the purpose of a county jail, will be able to weather the present winter.*
>
> *The fact that her timbers are in exceedingly bad condition was long since discovered and has been noticed on several occasions by grand juries.*
>
> *The subject should be considered by the Board of Supervisors and some other depot selected for the prisoners. It would not surprise us should the old craft be riddled by drifting logs sometime during the winter and sink at an inconvenient place like her predecessor the Stirling.*

In April, 1853, a tax was levied to finance a new jail. Before construction could be started, the Courthouse burned. It was decided to build a combination jail and court house.

The new jail-courthouse was completed in 1855 at 7th and I streets.

The end of Sacramento's floating jail house era arrived with the heavy rains of November 1859.

> *About six o'clock yesterday morning (November 18) the officers of La Grange were aroused by cry of prisoners, that the vessel was sinking, the water flowing in freely, and partially flooding cells between decks.*
>
> *The vessel sank sufficiently to admit water into the lumber hole forward, rendering it inadvisable to continue prisoners below, so they were admitted upon deck and closely watched till about a quarter of four p.m.*
>
> *They were by concerted action of the sheriff, chief of police, and supervisors, transferred to the Station house, 33 prisoners in all, including two females.*

By the time prison officials realized what was happening, it was too late to release the *La Grange* from its moorings.

The *La Grange* was held securely in place as the swirling waters closed over the ship until only the peak of its superstructure and two small flagpoles showed above water.

By the time the waters subsided, sand and sediment filled La Grange's hold and cabin. Whatever remained of *La Grange* after being salvaged was finished by the great flood of 1861-62.

174

Chapter 31

Outlying Towns

Auburn

Man's presence in Auburn dates back to 1400 B.C. The first known people were the Nisenan, an offshoot of the Maidu Tribe.

European settlers, hunters, trappers and fur traders appeared in the Auburn Ravine in the 1840s. They were followed by explorer-surveyor John Fremont in 1843-44, and by Theodore Sigard in 1845.

A young Frenchman by the name of Claude Chana settled on Sigard's Ranch on the Bear River. While still at Sigard's ranch, Chana learned of James Marshall's gold discovery at Coloma.

Chana, himself, found gold in the Auburn Ravine on May 16, 1848. By April 1849, North Fork Dry Diggings was a well-established mining camp. It was officially named Auburn in August 1849.

Auburn officially became a city when the Central Pacific Railroad made it one of their regular stops. By the turn of the century, Auburn had a population of about 2,000 people.

Carmichael

Daniel W. Carmichael came to California in 1885. He developed Carmichael Colony Number 1 on 1909 on 2,000 acres. The site was part of the Rancho San Juan Mexican land grant.

Carmichael later bought another 1,000 acres which was part of the Rancho Del Paso land grant which he called Colony Number 2.

Elk Grove

This early photo shows Elk Grove's Main Street.

Elk Grove was established in 1850 as a stage stop. Just 15 miles south of Sutter's Fort, Elk Grove became a hub for local commerce.

Elk Grove House was built in 1850 by James Hall, the founder of Elk Grove. Elk Grove House was reputed to be one of the finest stage stops between Sacramento and Stockton.

In 1972 Elk Grove had no stop lights, no fast food restaurants and a population of less than 11,000 people. Today, it is one of the fastest growing cities in California.

Fair Oaks

Fair Oaks is part of the Sacramento-Arden-Arcade-Roseville Metropolitan Statistical area.

Fair Oaks is bounded on the south side by the American River and Rancho Cordova. It is bounded on the north by Citrus Heights and on the West by Carmichael.

The area is known for its chickens. They run wild all over the village. The chickens inhabit the two small parks in the old town area and can often be seen fighting, begging for scraps, or roosting on playground equipment.

The community began as part of the 1844 Rancho San Juan Mexican land grant. In 1895, Brevet Brigadier General Charles Henry Howard and James W. Wilson of the Howard-Wilson Publishing Company of Chicago acquired rights to present Fair Oaks community.

The Howard-Wilson company surveyed and mapped the land. It began promoting Fair Oaks as one of their Sunset Colonies.

Roseville

Roseville's volunteer fire department.

In 1864, the Central Pacific Railroad's tracks were constructed eastward from Sacramento, and when they crossed a small Central Railroad Line, the spot was called "Junction". Junction eventually became known as Roseville.

Roseville's beginnings date back to the Gold Rush Days when discouraged miners took up farming along the rich creek bottoms.

Among the pioneer settlers was Martin A. Schellhous, who came to California with his wife. He acquired a 240-acre ranch. He stocked it with a number of cattle he had brought with him from

Michigan. His apple orchards and vineyards were among the first in Placer County.

Another pioneer rancher was young Walter F. Fiddyment. He and his wife, Elizabeth Jane Crawford Fiddyment arrived in California in 1854 and initially settled in Elk Grove.

Elizabeth Fiddyment reunited with her sister near present-day Roseville. Two years later, with her new husband, George Hill, she settled in the Pleasant Grove District.

Fiddyment family descendents still reside in Roseville.

Meet the Author

Alton Pryor

Alton Pryor has published fifty-plus books since turning 70 in 1997—many of them about California's past and the colorful characters who rode our trails to fame or infamy.

To date he has sold more than 180,000-plus copies of his first book, "Little Known Tales in California History", and has done respectably well with most of his other titles.

But until fate derailed his 33-year journalism career, he never aspired to write a book, and certainly never anticipated he would come to be regarded as "Mr. Self-Publishing" by his peers in the Sacramento area. "I would have liked living in the Old West," he says. "I wanted, at one time, to be a really good cowboy. I had horses as a young man and even took a raw colt and trained it to work cattle."

But, by the time Pryor was born on March 19, 1927, the era of gunslingers and gold miners was over, and he started life, instead, on his family's farm outside of King City in the Salinas Valley.

He was terminated after writing for 27 years for a magazine. The magazine was sold to a midwest firm.

Pryor turned to writing books and says now, "I wish I had been fired 20 years earlier."

Index

www.ingramcontent.com/pod-product-compliance
Lightning Source LLC
LaVergne TN
LVHW051521080426
835509LV00017B/2150